MERE CHRISTIANS

MERE CHRISTIANS

Inspiring Stories of Encounters with C. S. Lewis

EDITED BY
Mary Anne Phemister
and Andrew Lazo

a division of Baker Publishing Group
Grand Rapids, Michigan

Published by Baker Books
a division of Baker Publishing Group
P.O. Box 6287, Grand Rapids, MI 49516-6287
www.bakerbooks.com

Printed in the United States of America

Library of Congress Cataloging-in-Publication Data
Mere Christians : inspiring stories of encounters with C. S. Lewis / edited by Mary Anne Phemister and Andrew Lazo.
p. cm.
ISBN 978-0-8010-7184-3 (pbk.)
1. Christian biography. 2. Lewis, C. S. (Clive Staples), 1898–1963—Influence. I. Phemister, Mary Anne. II. Lazo, Andrew.
BR1702.M47 2009
270.8′20922—dc22 2008037974
[B]

In keeping with biblical principles of creation stewardship, Baker Publishing Group advocates the responsible use of our natural resources. As a member of the Green Press Initiative, our company uses recycled paper when possible. The text paper of this book is comprised of 30% post-consumer waste.

To Bill
and
To Susan

Contents

Foreword

Walter Hooper

Shortly after C. S. Lewis died, his friend Dr. Austin Farrer said to me, "You were fortunate that the man whose writings you admired so much was as likeable as his books. It might *not*, you know, have worked out that way. Suppose you had been an admirer of the books of Evelyn Waugh and met *him*!" Waugh, as everyone knew, was a man of colossal rudeness.

Austin Farrer's comment came to mind as I read over this fascinating book and discovered how many lives—including my own—have been enormously and permanently changed by C. S. Lewis. While reading the essays, I wondered if the lives of the authors would have changed as much if they had *met* Lewis? Would a meeting with Lewis have made any difference to what they got from his books?

I have no doubt that if Lewis read these words, he would have had me point to a passage in *The Personal Heresy* in which he said: "I must look where [the writer] looks and not turn round to face him. I must make of him not a spectacle but a pair of spectacles." He believed a book should be judged on its own merits rather than how much it tells us about the author.

Let us grant that a book should stand or fall by its own merits. Even so, if a reader happens to know the author of his or her favorite books—and Lewis knew quite a few authors, most notably J. R. R. Tolkien—the reader will find that the reading of these books is colored by the acquaintance of the author. The friends of Lewis that I've met all liked *him*, regardless of what they thought of his books. And those readers who met him liked him as much as they liked his books, and for the same reasons.

Except for Joy Davidman and Clyde Kilby, Thomas Howard and I are the only contributors to this volume who had the good fortune to meet C. S. Lewis. What effect did meeting him have on my enjoyment of his books? Do all the others represented in these pages understand his works less well because they never met him?

I was overwhelmed when I first came across Lewis's writings in 1953, and until we met ten years later I wanted very much merely to see him, although I never imagined I would have the chance. When that chance finally came in June 1963 and I rang the doorbell of The Kilns, I was terrified. I soon forgot my fear when Lewis invited me in for tea and we talked. Hours later, when he escorted me to the bus stop, I was sad that what I imagined would be a single meeting was ending. But Lewis invited me back to see him many times, and he eventually asked me to become his secretary and move into his house. In the preface and some of the letters in *The Collected Letters of C. S. Lewis, Volume III*, I mention that I went back to the United States at the end of the summer, with the intention of joining Lewis in January 1964, but sadly those plans were never realized because of Lewis's sudden death on November 22, 1963. However, I cannot complain. I expected to meet him only once, and I feel nothing but gratitude for his great and unexpected kindness.

Did those months with Lewis effect any further change in me other than that already made by his books? That is a question Lewis would have been eager to answer. After we'd come to know each other, he invited me to call him "Jack," and for a while he was almost like two people: the author of my favorite books, and Jack Lewis, the friend who would never speak of his own work unless I pressed him. Quoting one of his books one day, I suddenly realized how it must have sounded to him. "As C. S. Lewis has said," I began; "Oh, but you *are* C. S. Lewis!" Thereafter he made it a joke between us, and whenever he wanted something done, he would say, for example, "As C. S. Lewis has said, 'I would like a pot of tea.' As C. S. Lewis has said, '*You* will go and make it.'"

To turn from the printed page to the author of those pages was an exhilarating experience. However, from the first day we met I noticed how *exactly* Lewis sounded like his books. Even he could not always find fresh ways of phrasing something, and I remember him saying some things precisely as they are found in his books.

The main difference was that, whereas his books say what they say and that is it, his conversation was, to quote Hebrews 4:12, "quick, and powerful, and sharper than any twoedged sword." Woe betide anyone who entered into a conversation with Lewis frivolously, expecting to break it off when he or she was tired of thinking. "Have we *finished* talking about that?" Lewis asked when I tried to wiggle out of some hard thinking on a subject I had raised. But who could be such a fool as not to want to learn from C. S. Lewis, who was always arguing toward some truth. Lewis was at his best in the meetings of the Inklings I attended. On those occasions I was reminded of the scene in *That Hideous Strength* when the god of language, Mercury, descended on St Anne's. Like Jane Studdock, I had never heard "such eloquence, such melody, . . . such toppling structures of double meaning, such skyrockets of metaphor and allusion." Unfortunately, it was impossible afterwards to remember what they said.

How different are Lewis's *writings*—as memorable and as quotable as the King James Version of the Bible. I will be forever grateful that I had the double pleasure of Lewis's company and his writings. But, as Lewis would have wished, it is his writings that will outlast memories of him; they are the rich fruits of his remarkable mind. Knowing Lewis for a few months will almost certainly remain the climax of my life; on the other hand, I don't think the authors who contributed to this volume understand Lewis's works *less* well because they never met him. As Lewis said in one of his letters, "An author doesn't necessarily understand the meaning of his own story better than anyone else." If God has been working through the writings of C. S. Lewis, which certainly seems to be true, I would not be surprised if those whose lives have been changed by Lewis have brought back treasures he never knew about.

Walter Hooper is an eminent Lewis scholar, literary adviser to the estate of C. S. Lewis, and editor of *The Collected Letters of C. S. Lewis*.

Preface

MARJORIE LAMP MEAD

In this volume, *Mere Christians*, the editors have gathered the reflections of diverse individuals whose lives have been significantly influenced by the words of C. S. Lewis. Not surprisingly, despite all of the differences in these varied accounts, there is a common thread of gratitude running throughout. Lewis himself understood the deep indebtedness that a reader often feels for the words of an author. He expressed it this way in *An Experiment in Criticism*:

> Those of us who have been true readers all our life seldom fully realise the enormous extension of our being which we owe to authors. We realise it best when we talk with an unliterary friend. He may be full of goodness and good sense but he inhabits a tiny world. In it, we should be suffocated. The man who is contented to be only himself, and therefore less a self, is in prison. My own eyes are not enough for me, I will see through those of others.

Just as other writers acted as noteworthy guides for Lewis in his imaginative and spiritual pilgrimage, so too has Lewis served as literary mentor to numerous individuals. The contributors to this book underline some of the reasons why Lewis was so important in their lives, variously describing his writings as authentic, strikingly clear, approachable, intellectually and imaginatively invigorating, transparent, humble, and infused with joy. Author and broadcaster Anne Atkins offers a particularly apt observation on the potency of Lewis's words: "[In his works] he has done that humble thing which the greatest writers do and the lesser ones neglect: he has done the work for me. He has gone to the trouble of making his ideas accessible, and simple, and clear as a summer sky. He makes the life of the reader easy."

The impact of Lewis's published works upon the personal lives of some of his readers was so great that they wrote him letters expressing their appreciation and often asking further questions. Even though this extensive correspondence eventually became a heavy burden upon his time, nonetheless, Lewis faithfully answered each letter. In looking at these responses, we find indications of how he viewed his role as literary mentor. Certainly, there was an obedient selflessness about his willingness to help his readers. For example, he made the following offer to a correspondent who had just become a Christian: "Blessings on you and a hundred thousand welcomes. Make use of me in any way you please." There was also a genuine humility in how he viewed the significance of his own influence, even telling one reader (whom he was counseling about questions of faith): "As for my part in it, remember that anybody (or any *thing*) may be used by the Holy Spirit as a conductor. I say this not so much for modesty as to guard against any danger of your feeling that, when the shine goes out of my books (as it will) that the *real thing* is in any way involved. *It* mustn't fade when I do." But most important to note, Lewis's intention was not to convert his readers to a particular way of belief or even to encourage them to become adherents of his own works; rather, his central purpose was always to direct readers to the person of Jesus Christ. Indeed, when one group of readers became a bit too enthusiastic in their regard for his writings, Lewis firmly cautioned: "I am shocked to think that your friends think of following *me*. I wanted them to follow Christ. But they'll get over this confusion soon, I trust." With this in mind, I believe that Lewis would be pleased by the pieces gathered in this collection. The heartfelt appreciation of the contributors notwithstanding, it is evident that their gratitude is ultimately for their life-changing encounter with the divine as Lewis primarily intended. Undoubtedly, this is true for many others as well. Through the clarity and power of his words, C. S. Lewis has faithfully served both to open his readers' imaginations and to challenge their intellects—resulting in countless changed lives.

Marjorie Lamp Mead is associate director of the Marion E. Wade Center and coauthor of *A Reader's Guide through the Wardrobe* and *C. S. Lewis Letters to Children*.

Acknowledgments

We gratefully thank all the contributors who wrote their stories, especially Jerry Root, who was most helpful in guiding us to individuals whose lives have been transformed through reading C. S. Lewis. Of course we owe untold thanks to the staff at the Marion E. Wade Center especially to Chris Mitchell, Marj Mead, Heidi Truty, and Laura Schmidt, who have helped us in so many ways by their willingness to direct us to others that Jerry may have missed, and by their deep knowledge, ready wisdom, and constant good cheer in guiding us in Lewis matters in general.

We are indebted to the enthusiastic encouragement of Walter Hooper, David Downing, Phillip Yancey, Joseph Pearce, and Doug and Merrie Gresham, and to the many friends and family who helped us to bring these inspiring accounts to a broader audience.

Andrew would like to thank the Caffeinated Lamp-post Society; Stan Mattson and the staff of the C. S. Lewis Foundation; Amber Salladin, Malcolm Guite, and Diana Pavlac Glyer (kindred spirits); Phil Keaggy; Frs. Tom Reeder, Jim Nutter, and Mark Crawford; Toni Nettles; and his father Javier Lazo López for their invaluable contributions to making Lewis come alive.

And finally, we wish to thank the editorial, production, and marketing staffs at the Baker Publishing Group, especially Bob Hosack and Mary Wenger, for their dedicated and skillful work in guiding us through the publishing process.

Introduction

Mary Anne Phemister

Although millions have read C. S. Lewis's books and have found themselves deeply touched by his words, few have written down their personal accounts. I volunteer as a docent at Wheaton College's Marion E. Wade Center, the world's foremost archive and repository of material relating to C. S. Lewis and six other like-minded writers: J. R. R. Tolkien, Dorothy L. Sayers, George MacDonald, G. K. Chesterton, Charles Williams, and Owen Barfield. I often ask visitors, "Which one of these seven British authors particularly interests you?" One woman's response planted the seed that has grown into the book you now hold.

"C. S. Lewis changed my life!" Dorothy Karabin replied without a moment's hesitation. When I asked her how Lewis had done that, she briefly summarized her story, specifically citing the reading of a passage in *Mere Christianity* as her defining moment. Her story reminded me of Chuck Colson's conversion account in *Born Again*. These two vastly different individuals—one a nurse, the other a prominent former adviser to President Nixon—both became convicted of their pride and self-conceit by a book written by an author whom neither had heard of before. As a result of their reading, both experienced profound, life-changing encounters with God.

I asked Mrs. Karabin if she would write down her story. And as I continued to ask this question and to collect people's written responses, I soon discovered that C. S. Lewis's *Mere Christianity*, along with most of his other forty-five books, has given rise to a kind of quiet revolution in the spiritual lives of countless people.

Many of the contributors to this anthology first found Lewis as children through his Chronicles of Narnia. Stephen Savage, Nick Seward, and Mark Stibbe recall their subtle wooing into the reality of Christianity by the lordly Aslan. Tom Arthur, Ronald Bresland, and Colin Duriez discovered Narnia as adults. Still others came through the door via the cosmic trilogy. James Como and David Lyle Jeffrey both found in *An Experiment in Criticism* ideas that challenged and changed their thinking and teaching. Lewis died November 22, 1963, one week shy of his sixty-fifth birthday and the same day that President Kennedy was assassinated. Now, nearly half a century later, Lewis's books remain in print both in English and translated into dozens of languages, continuing to find their way into the hands of millions of readers around the world.

Lewis served as my great counselor during my pediatric rotation while I was training to become a nurse. I wrestled with how a good God could allow innocent children to suffer such pain and disfigurement. Then a friend gave me *The Problem of Pain*. Lewis reminded me that pain arises from the evil in the world and formed no part of God's plan for us. There are just some things God cannot change, at least not just now. Nevertheless, Christians *must* try to prevent and alleviate pain and suffering, however and whenever we can. I thus discovered in Lewis the strong encouragement to make myself into the best nurse I could be and to serve God with the gifts he had given me. And I also found Lewis urging me to consider that pain and suffering can have a character-building effect, not just on the caregiver but also on the innocent children and their parents who suffer in various ways. The problem of pain still annoys me, but I must trust that God knows what is best. The final answer I must leave to heaven—yet another mystery of faith I must face. I found myself, however, strangely reassured by Lewis's explanations and Scripture references. He reminded me that "the sufferings of this present time are not worth comparing with the glory that is to be revealed to us" (Rom. 8:18 RSV).

Thousands more could have contributed to this volume, but that would have made a book too laborious for us to assemble and far too heavy for you to hold. However, I am enormously grateful to those who have shared their experiences of how C. S. Lewis has transformed their lives. Because I love to listen to people tell the stories of their spiritual journeys, I find the gathering of these accounts deeply satisfying. Perhaps because of this book others will now share their stories. We haven't told even a tenth part of these tales, and we would love to hear from you.

Mary Anne Phemister is a docent at the Marion E. Wade Center.

Introduction

Andrew Lazo

When trying to assess the sheer size of the impact of a writer such as C. S. Lewis, one immediately faces an insurmountable challenge: what can we possibly use to measure such a thing? There are millions of Google hits, millions of books sold and continuing to sell (in some cases faster than ever), and more than a billion dollars in movie tickets sold. A constant stream of Lewis quotations flows from writers, thinkers, ministers, and scholars, and there is a vast selection of books about various aspects of his life. All of these facts offer a start but seem merely to scratch the surface. This book uses another approach, providing a sampling of the startlingly wide variety of lives Lewis has touched as a kind of spiritual mentor, a wise guide further up in the faith who can still influence others with his wisdom, humility, and that old-fashioned word *piety*. Although most of the contributors have encountered Lewis only through his writings, such a meeting has offered to them (along with millions of others) many ideas they have spent a lifetime grappling with. For example, Lewis's argument that the Moral Law argues for the possibility of a personal and omnipotent God continues to convince. The clearness of his logic and crispness of his style will obviously endure, carrying his message to this and future generations.

My own story mirrors many in this book. As a boy, whenever a package would come from Aunt Ingrid for Christmas or my birthday, my eyes would light up. One year she included a set of the Chronicles of Narnia. In all the ways that mattered most when I was a child, my imagination came alive as I turned page after page. These books made me into a lifelong reader.

Years later, while living in Nashville, I became friends with the guitarist Phil Keaggy. Talk often turned to our reading, and one day Phil lent me a book he had just finished. Little did either of us know that when he handed me *Letters to an American Lady*, he had sealed my fate. Lewis's tough, terse prose wholly absorbed me and swept me away into a sea of good humor, stern virtue, and clear good sense. I began then a path on which I still find myself—reading and studying everything I can by and about Lewis. I found, too, that the Narnian adventures that had delighted me as a boy took on a whole new meaning as I read them with eyes of an informed faith.

Like many contributors to this book, Lewis came to me at a crucial time of doubt in my faith. I found in him the kind of rigorous rationalism that helped me to see Christianity as the most reasonable approach to the world I encountered outside and within myself. Until I read Lewis, I had never known how to combine the best thinking and the deepest believing. Indeed, I had begun to despair that it was possible.

And then Lewis came bounding in. As I read *God in the Dock*, *Surprised by Joy*, and more collections of his letters, I soon found in Lewis a man who had thought through his atheism far more thoroughly than I had ever thought through my faith. I don't exaggerate in claiming that Lewis taught me how to think. In fact, I gladly claim that when I was a child, Lewis sparked my imaginative life, and when I became a man, Lewis saved my intellectual life.

Lewis continues to do this for me—to spark, to save, to clarify my thinking, and to challenge my mode of life—mentoring me in countless ways. His example encourages me to think, to speak, and to write with the utmost clarity I can manage. His constant devotion and intense humility encourage me to grapple with my own flaws and to live each day as if it makes an eternal difference. As George MacDonald had become for him, Lewis has become my master, a trustworthy guide through my life.

In *The Four Loves* Lewis describes how friends huddle around a shared interest and how the very essence of friendship lies in the discovery that someone else cares as deeply about the same truths. This glad group of people changed by reading C. S. Lewis find in him not merely a powerful influence for good but also a faithful teacher, evangelist, apologist, and counselor. C. S. Lewis offers himself as a guide to things that echo in the core of each of us. His help on our paths rings out true, glad, and clear.

Andrew Lazo holds an M.A. in literature from Rice University. He teaches literature at the University of Houston and is an independent speaker and scholar on the life and works of C. S. Lewis.

C. S. Lewis (1898–1963)

A Brief Biography of an Extraordinary Life

Andrew Lazo

The First Ten Years: A Happy Boyhood

Clive Staples Lewis was born in Belfast, Northern Ireland, on November 29, 1898, to Albert and Flora Lewis, who already had an older son, Warren ("Warnie"). A bright and self-possessed boy, Lewis enjoyed a happy childhood. He delighted in his home life, which included loving parents, a nurse who sparked his imagination with Irish fairy tales, and a close friendship with Warnie, with whom Lewis created stories of clothed animals in an imaginary land they called "Boxen." One day Warnie brought him a toy garden he had made on a biscuit tin. As he looked at that lovely, tiny garden, Lewis felt for the first time a stab of longing for beauty. He called this feeling "joy," and the pursuit of it formed a major theme in his life. This happy life of books, stories, and the Irish countryside continued until his mother died of cancer in 1908. Lewis was just nine years old.

The Next Ten Years: Learning and Losing Faith

As a young man, Lewis began to write poetry while continuing to read many of the hundreds of books he discovered both in his home and at bookshops and in bookseller's catalogs. Lewis's unhappiness in the private school setting led Albert Lewis to send his son to study with a private tutor for nearly three years, an environment in which Lewis thrived. W. T. Kirkpatrick taught him classics as well as the rigorous rationality that would later characterize both Lewis's academic career and his approach to faith. Lewis loved the routine and the challenges Kirkpatrick set for him, and during this time three patterns emerged. First, Lewis became a writer, maintaining an extensive correspondence with friends and family and writing a great deal of poetry. Second, he read everything he could get his hands on, including Norse and Arthurian mythology and the books of George MacDonald. And third, he lost his faith, gladly setting it aside for an enthusiastic atheism. His work with Kirkpatrick won him admission to Oxford University, but before he began his studies, World War I intervened. On his nineteenth birthday, in November 1917, Lewis arrived at the front line in France's Somme Valley.

Lewis in the Twenties: Scholarship, Friendship, and Fledgling Faith

Lewis served as a lieutenant until he was injured in battle; he convalesced in England for the rest of the war. Earlier, he had agreed that should anything happen to his friend and fellow soldier Paddy Moore, Lewis would take care of Paddy's mother. Lewis kept that promise, living with Mrs. Moore for the rest of her life. Their puzzling relationship appears to have started as a romance, but after his conversion Lewis came to call her his "mother." After the war ended, Lewis pursued his Oxford education in earnest, achieving rare success. In four years Lewis completed three degrees (in philosophy, classics, and English), each time taking the highest possible honors. Following these years of successful study, Lewis won a job as a tutor in English at Magdalen College, Oxford, a post that he held for nearly thirty years. His responsibilities included lecturing, writing scholarly articles and books, and tutoring individual students, and he enjoyed enormous popularity and success in his work. Also during these years Lewis made several important friends, including J. R. R. Tolkien, Owen Barfield, and Hugo Dyson, who challenged his atheism and helped lead him back to faith. These friends walked together, argued, and shared their writings with each other, and over time they helped Lewis begin to doubt his own doubts about the existence of God. At age twenty-nine Lewis very reluctantly converted to theism. In 1933 Lewis took one final step toward faith, converting from mere theism to Christianity. Much to his surprise, he soon discovered that the joy he had pursued all his life came from Christ. He remained convinced of the truth of Christianity throughout his life, and in many ways his life began to open up for him once he took this step.

Thriving in the Thirties: Conversion, Inklings, and Scholarly Success

In 1930, along with Warnie and Mrs. Moore, Lewis bought The Kilns, his home for the rest of his life. Upon retiring from his career as a military officer, Warnie moved into The Kilns to stay. Having failed at his lifelong ambition to be a poet, Lewis turned to scholarly work and found enormous critical success with his first scholarly book, *The Allegory of Love*. That book won him the attention of the editors of the Oxford History of English Literature, who asked him to write volume three, on the nondramatic writing of the 1500s. It took Lewis nine years to finish the volume, which scholars still read today. Along with Tolkien and other like-minded friends, Lewis founded the Inklings, a writing community that met weekly to read aloud from their own manuscripts in progress. This group produced a number of works, including Tolkien's The Lord of the Rings, Lewis's Cosmic Trilogy, and many others. The books that came out of these meetings marked the beginning for Lewis of a string of successful popular writings that continued almost uninterrupted until his death.

The Forties: Apologist, Author, and Several Sorts of Endings

During the 1940s, Lewis enjoyed a great deal of success and increasing fame, although some of this worked against him. He took up the role which made him most famous, that of defending the Christian faith. During World War II Lewis gave a series of talks on the BBC explaining Christianity. These lectures, which eventually became *Mere Christianity*, made Lewis's the second most-recognized voice in England, after that of Winston Churchill. He also published several books arguing for the reasonableness of the Christian faith, along with the phenomenally popular *The Screwtape Letters*. That book landed him on the cover of *Time* magazine and in some ways sealed his professional fate. Many Oxford colleagues despised the fact that Lewis published popular books about theology, a topic that fell outside his chosen field of English literature. Lewis also became a very outspoken and public Christian, and the backlash likely cost him three professorships. Nevertheless, Lewis's reputation continued to rise as he published a number of books and essays during this period. He continued writing fiction that explored his interests in mythology and faith. This decade of Lewis's life also saw many things come to an end. Fellow Inkling Charles Williams died unexpectedly in 1945. The Inklings stopped meeting to read their work to each other in 1949, and finally, Mrs. Moore died in 1950, freeing Lewis from the burden of caring for her. Exhausted on many levels, Lewis felt as though his creative gifts were at an end. Little did he imagine the great joys and successes that awaited him in his fifties.

The Fifties: Surprised by Narnia, Cambridge, and Joy

Lewis could scarcely have envisioned the gains that would soon succeed his losses. Within three years Lewis completed his work on the Oxford History of English Literature, compiled the BBC broadcasts into *Mere Christianity*, penned his spiritual autobiography *Surprised by Joy*, and worked on a book on prayer. In his "spare" time and mostly for his own amusement, Lewis wrote all seven Narnian Chronicles, which were published, one per year, from 1950 to 1957. These fairy tales enjoyed enormous success, finding an enthusiastic and enduring audience. Clearly Lewis's creative gifts had not abandoned him. Professional success soon followed as well. Cambridge, in an almost unprecedented move, created a professorship in medieval and Renaissance literature specifically for Lewis, in part to undo the injustices he had undergone at Oxford. Though initially he had to be persuaded to accept the post, Lewis delighted in his new university, along with the freedom to write that this new post afforded him. And much to his surprise, Lewis also found love. Joy Davidman, an American Jewish poet and a former atheist, had come to faith in part through Lewis's books. In 1950 the two began a lively correspondence. In 1952 they met in person when Joy visited and eventually moved to England, and by 1956 Lewis and Joy had become fast friends. In 1956, when the British government refused to grant her permission to remain in England, Lewis married Joy in a civil ceremony in order to extend his citizenship to her and her two young sons, David and Douglas. They continued to live in separate houses, but their friendship grew closer. Before long their civil marriage, which at first had seemed to Lewis only an act of charity, blossomed into romance for them both. In 1957 Lewis and Joy were married in a religious ceremony in Joy's hospital room, for she had fallen desperately ill with cancer, and they thought she would soon die. But a miraculous remission gave the couple three happy years together before the cancer returned. Joy died on July 13, 1960, ending a remarkable decade for Lewis. Having lost Mrs. Moore, Charles Williams, and the Inklings, Lewis found friendship, family, and love with Joy in the last years of their lives. He found professional ease and respect with his Cambridge professorship. He also rediscovered his authorial gifts and wrote many of his best and most enduring books in this decade, including the strange and magnificent *Till We Have Faces*, a book inspired and encouraged by Joy.

The Sixties: Lastly Letting Go

During the last three years of his life, Lewis continued to enjoy his role at Cambridge and his friends, although poor health due to kidney problems limited his activities. Still, Lewis continued working, publishing a number of books, including *A Grief Observed*, an account of his grief over losing Joy. Lewis did his best to raise his stepsons, making a lasting impression on both boys, especially Douglas, who has written about his years with Lewis (*Lenten Lands*). By 1963 his failing health forced him to resign his Cambridge post. In July of that year, Lewis had a heart attack and slipped into a coma, but he recovered, remaining alert into the autumn. At 5:30 p.m. on November 22, 1963, Lewis passed away due to kidney failure and a weakened heart. He died an hour and a half before the assassination of John F. Kennedy, one week before his sixty-fifth birthday. All who knew Lewis describe him as a man of quick wit and constant laughter, profound and deliberate humility, enormous learning and intelligence, and as a man thoroughly converted to the claims of Jesus Christ on his extraordinary life.

1

Love and an Evangelized Intellect

Atessa Afshar

Iran—land of Cyrus and Darius and Esther and the Ayatollah. Land, also, of my birth. The year I was born, C. S. Lewis died. But I would have cared nothing for that, then. It was the last decade of the Shah's reign. Under his influence, Tehran had grown explosively, owing its identity too much to Western ways to be truly Middle Eastern. But Iranian history and tradition lingered in every corner, so that it couldn't become truly Western either.

I was born in a nominally Muslim family. Nominal Muslims differ little from nominal Christians. My parents believed in being generally conscientious; they were only-tell-white-lies, law-abiding citizens. However, they did not adhere to even the most basic tenets of Islam. My mother would not be caught dead wearing the Hijab (the traditional Muslim covering for women) outside of special religious occasions. She was an extremely fashionable woman, as were most of her friends. My mother was a true Tehrani, as comfortable sitting in her yellow Camaro as she was cross-legged on the floor, quoting Omar Khayam.

My father, a Paris-educated radiologist, was a general in the army of the Shah, though I think of him more as a physician than a military man. We never could figure out how he came by the row of medals on his dress uniform.

Although by no means a religious man, he respected spiritual things in his own way. The few deep conversations I recall having with my father stick in my mind like Super Glue, such as when he told me to give God his due respect. My parents had rejected much of Islam, but not the notion of a loving God. Like Christians, Muslims believe that God is loving and compassionate, but they have no proof of that claim—no manger and no cross to back up their beliefs. As proudly educated Tehranis, they had abandoned the more quaint points of religion long ago: devils and angels and miracles were the domain of the ignorant.

I mostly learned about Islam and its tenets from my grandmother, a devout Muslim. She prayed at least five times a day, fasted one month out of the year, made the pilgrimage to Mecca, wore the Hijab, paid her tithe, and followed Mohammed's teachings with all her might. But her belief did not seem to have the intellectual depth to satisfy my questions. Once I asked my grandmother if God had created space itself, then *where* was he before space was there? "Never ask that question or any like it," my grandmother admonished. "Such questions are sinful." I thought, *If God is that oversensitive, I'm not sure we'll get along.*

I needed a God who could withstand my questions and more. There was no C. S. Lewis in my world to answer the challenges of my mind. Not until years later would Lewis's writings teach me that to love God does not require you to get an annulment from your brain. Lewis would one day teach me that God isn't afraid of our challenges. He questioned God with more ruthless vigor than anything my mind could summon. Yet he came away increased in his faith.

When I was almost fourteen years old, about a year before the Islamic Revolution, my parents divorced, and my mother decided to leave Iran and settle in Europe with my sister and me. Little did we know when we moved to Cambridge, England, that Iran would never again be our home. Cambridge, coincidentally, was Lewis's last academic home. I must have walked by Lewis's college many times, never knowing that it once housed a genius and a man of faith, who one day would aid my own journey to God.

Moving to a different country is always jarring. Different food, different customs, and a different language can all become overwhelming. I remember one of the first things that took getting used to was the cemeteries. I had never seen a cemetery as a child growing up in Iran.

Death is not a thing you stare at in the Middle East. People rarely make a will, because it makes death seem too uncomfortably close. One never speaks of the death of someone still living, not even under the most pragmatic or respectful of contexts. Cemeteries are built in out-of-the-way places, where you aren't likely to happen upon one by chance. As a child, I never wore black or visited the graveside of dead relatives and friends.

I think this avoidance of death comes from the fact that Islam offers very few eternal guarantees. One enters paradise by the merit of one's actions and obedience to Allah. Because there is no notion of grace—of sins covered by God's own sacrificial death—human death remains the unconquered enemy no one likes to be reminded of. Funerals are emotional trials; the loss seems so great that one can receive almost no comfort.

Conversely, Christ conquered death. It has no sting. Years later, when I first read the Narnia Chronicles and found that the children died in a train crash, I did not even feel sad. Before Lewis, reading a book about likable teenagers who die in the end would have brought me to fears and tears. But in Narnia, Lewis made the afterlife so real and natural that death lost its clammy hold of fear upon me. Why be sad when they were with Aslan?

In England, I began to attend a girls' boarding school called Princess Helena College. There I went to church for the first time, for weekly church attendance is part of English heritage.

I didn't get much out of those Sunday pilgrimages, and it was probably mostly my own fault. The few foreign girls who attended the school were told to sit upstairs and read their own holy books. I read—romance novels! So while I learned some things about love, it wasn't exactly what Jesus had in mind.

Eventually I moved to the States to go to college, and this has been my home since. It still shocks me, however, that having lived in the Christian West most of my adult life, I never heard the gospel until I was twenty-six years old. Perhaps people did not want to intrude or offend. Perhaps they just did not know how to approach me.

Finally, I think God decided he had had enough. If Christians were not going to approach me, then he would have to do it directly! During a particularly difficult time of my life, I had a dream that, as I stood by the Sea of Galilee, Jesus himself walked toward me. Having never read the Bible, my only real knowledge of Jesus had been through films I had seen as a schoolgirl. Perhaps you know the ones I mean: the ones in which Jesus was blond, blue-eyed, and very handsome in a movie-star kind of way. None of this was true of the Jesus in my dream. Frankly, he appeared quite homely to me. Not until later did I read in Isaiah that the Messiah would not be much to look at.

My first reaction was disappointment. *This* was Jesus? Perhaps the most miraculous part of this dream, however, apart from the fact that Jesus asked me to follow him and I did, was that I knew who he was—I was aware of the fullness of his identity. I knew that this man was the Son of God, very God of very God, and to be trusted above all. The dream did not make me a Christian. But it did give me three days of unshakable peace, a very precious commodity at that time in my life, and it also laid a foundation for what followed.

Within months of my dream, Christians finally began to share the message of salvation with me. In the Bible I came across a passage that began to change my heart. The text is one so familiar to most Christians that we may barely even give it a second thought. But 1 Corinthians 13 was a revelation to me. The heart of the teenager who had read all those romance novels still hungered for a deeper romance. All these years I had been looking for the perfect love, the love that would accept me, cherish me, complete me. It seemed at once impossible and healing to me, this love promised by God. I realized that I could not rise to these words by my own strength.

When I first said yes to Jesus, I still considered many biblical assertions naive. The "sophisticated" Tehrani in me could not swallow the idea of demons and angels and miracles. In short, such truths seemed too ridiculous to accept. One might as well believe in the tooth fairy.

But Lewis salvaged these spiritual truths from the cloying hold of cultural misrepresentations. In *Perelandra*, he displayed angels as close to their biblical revelation as words can manage. I was captivated: these *eldila* I could believe in, for they were not ridiculous, dewy-looking cherubs. I began to pray that God would give his *eldila* charge over me. Lewis's fictional vocabulary was more real to me than the culturally defunct words that had lost their biblical meaning in the twentieth century. Wormwood and his incompetent nephew, Screwtape, opened my mind to the fact that I had a real enemy. I began to ask God for protection from demonic influences, whereas before, I had thought of my own sin as the *only* enemy. With the Chronicles of

Narnia, my imagination awoke to the idea of a true heaven, and all my old beliefs about reincarnation simply fell away without a single argument. Lewis had managed to make eternal life so grippingly real that the fiction of reincarnation could not withstand the onslaught of the facts. C. S. Lewis didn't evangelize me, but he freed me to be a whole Christian, not one bound up by the lies of my old culture or the deceptions of my new one. Lewis made the worldview of Jesus real to me. I did not have to divorce my intellect from my faith, but merely to evangelize it.

Associate minister at First Church of Christ, Wethersfield, Connecticut, **Atessa Afshar** is one of only a few Iranian-born women working in full-time Christian ministry. Her B.A. degree is in English and biology; she holds an M.Div. from Yale Divinity School.

2

Learning to Love God While Fearing Him

Randy Alcorn

In 1969 I came to Christ as an unchurched teenager, my mind a blank slate for the things of God.

Soon I read my first C. S. Lewis book, *The Problem of Pain*. It was my wakeup call: being a Christian wouldn't allow me to ignore the world's problems; it would require me to face them. Lewis showed the way. He also gave me my first chapter on heaven, a subject that grew to become a central part of my life and writing. I can still hear him say, "Our Father refreshes us on the journey with some pleasant inns, but will not encourage us to mistake them for home."

Mere Christianity showed me that my faith needn't be blind, that it rested on a bedrock of historical events, and that it could be articulated with rational arguments. These points made sense to me, and soon I was trying them out on my friends. Again a memorable line: "I must keep alive in myself the desire for my true country, which I shall not find till after death."

One day in a Christian bookstore located in the garage of a private home, I discovered *Out of the Silent Planet*. Was this the same C. S.

Lewis who wrote the other books? *Science fiction?* I'd grown up on science fiction and had left it behind when I came to Christ. Could a Christian actually read science fiction? Could a Christian write it? Within a month I'd devoured *Perelandra* and *That Hideous Strength*. By then Lewis's fingerprints were all over me. If George MacDonald baptized Lewis's imagination, Lewis baptized mine.

Now, thirty years later, a barrister's bookcase in my office is filled with nothing but books by and about Lewis. On long, lonely nights when I ask myself if the work I do as a writer is worth it, their presence reminds me that it is. I have been so shaped by those books, so drawn to my Lord, that it fuels my hope that God will use my writing to change others, too.

I was in college when I discovered Narnia. Aslan overshadowed all. The Great Lion, son of the Emperor-beyond-the-Sea, unveiled Christ to me in fresh ways. Through Aslan, Lewis led me to a bigger and more biblically accurate view of Jesus, second member of the Triune God.

Aslan was not a tame lion. He was good, but not safe. Aslan unlocked the mystery of the "fear of God," which had been hard for me to harmonize with the love of God. Aslan proved that it wasn't just possible, but necessary—actually, wonderful—to love and fear God at the same time. Loving Aslan more every time he appeared, I grew to love Jesus more. In college I studied theology by day, but at night escaped into Narnia, which infused blood into the body of Christian doctrine.

I read *The Silver Chair* while facing the costs of following Christ. I understood why Jill begged the Lion to promise not to do anything to her if she came and drank from the river at his feet. He refused. She asked if he might eat her, and he said that he had swallowed boys and girls, cities and realms. "I dare not drink," she said. He replied, "Then you will die of thirst." And when she said she must find another stream, he spoke words still etched in my mind: "There is no other stream."

The lesson? I couldn't follow Christ on my terms. I had to follow him on his. He was the master. I was the servant. There could be no role reversal.

It was Lewis who convinced me that the same person could write good nonfiction and fiction, and emboldened me to try. All my books are touched by Lewis, because ultimately the books we write are the overflow of the books we've read.

In *The Four Loves* I learned about friendship. By then I knew what Lewis knew, that an author can become a friend, someone you can rejoin at will, picking up right where you left off. I look forward to meeting Jack Lewis and exploring the new earth, where there will be time for us all to walk and talk, with new friends who are also old friends, in the joyful presence of King Jesus.

Today God still uses Lewis to draw me further up and further in. My favorite paragraph, forever engraved on my heart—words found at the end of *The Last Battle*—is one of God's greatest gifts to me. I have read these words at many memorial services, and I hope that one day they will be read at mine.

> And for us this is the end of all the stories, and we can most truly say that they all lived happily ever after. But for them it was only the beginning of the real story. All their life in this world and all their adventures in Narnia had only been the cover and the title page: now at last they were beginning Chapter One of the Great Story which no one on earth has read: which goes on for ever: in which every chapter is better than the one before.

Randy Alcorn is the author of more than two dozen books, including *Heaven*, *The Treasure Principle*, and *Safely Home*. The director of Eternal Perspective Ministries (www.epm.org), he speaks widely and has taught at Multnomah Bible College and Western Seminary (Portland, Oregon). Randy and his wife, Nanci, live in Gresham, Oregon. They have two daughters and four grandsons.

3

Lewis Opened My Eyes

Mary DeKonty Applegate

The works of C. S. Lewis changed the lives of both my husband and me, but in completely different ways. In my case, I was reared in a strong fundamentalist community, where worldly knowledge was regarded as evil. This stance was especially difficult for someone attending a college preparatory high school requiring several science courses. Consequently, I learned to survive academically by memorizing information. My cycle of study consisted of memorization and regurgitation of facts, a cycle that continued throughout my four years at Evangel College in Springfield, Missouri. Unfortunately, my surface level of learning was mirrored by a surface level of spirituality. I had come to believe that the level of emotion that the relationship could elicit from me would accurately reflect the quality of my relationship with Christ.

Not long after I began my teaching career in public schools, I realized that although I loved my career and my students, I did not possess the knowledge and skills that I needed to help them achieve. I decided to pursue first a master's degree and then a doctorate in the field of reading. Despite my academic successes, I was still plagued by a sense of insecurity, acutely aware of my past rote learning and how much I had forgotten of what I had mastered solely for tests. And as I began to thrive in an atmosphere of academic challenges, I became much more aware of a nagging sense of what I perceived as the "intellectual softness" of Christianity. Eventually I began to walk as closely as possible on the road of secular humanism, the philosophy of choice for the intellectually elite.

In the summer of 1998, in the midst of my growing uneasiness, I began calling my brother, who was going through a difficult period in his life. During our weekly calls, I assumed that I was providing my brother with much-needed encouragement, yet soon it dawned on me that each time I spoke with him, I felt uplifted. I was struck by his comment that he was getting up early each day to spend time praying for the "sweet spirit of Christ." I suggested to my husband, Tony, that we should more actively pursue our own spiritual growth. He agreed with surprisingly little resistance, and off we headed to the nearest bookstore to find a book that we could read and discuss together.

After just a few minutes of searching, Tony suggested *Mere Christianity*, a book he had read twenty-five years earlier and one that he felt I might enjoy. As we began to read and to talk about our reactions to it, we found ourselves drawn to the logical seriousness of Lewis's faith. After we had devoured *Mere Christianity* many times over, we expanded our Lewis library to include *The Screwtape Letters*, *Miracles*, *The Problem of Pain*, *The Great Divorce*, the Space Trilogy, the Chronicles of Narnia, and anything else of Lewis's we could get our hands on. We also read an assortment of biographies, finding dozens of connections between Lewis's life and his ideas, connections that revealed how much he had truly become a teacher and spiritual guide for both of us.

The sheer fact that someone of Lewis's enormous intelligence and towering scholarly accomplishments shared my belief in Christ eliminated any concerns I had about the intellectual viability of the Christian faith. Lewis opened my eyes to the sometimes overwhelming complexity and rational challenge of Christianity. Here at last was a man who never shied away from even the thorniest of problems and whose presentation of Christianity enabled me to balance the demands of both intellect and emotion in my spiritual life.

Some time later I experienced an unfounded attack on my reputation that struck at the very heart of my professional insecurities. Only then did I discover the real impact of Lewis's teaching in my life. In the midst of my agitation, I was forced to come face to face with the realization that I had the type of pride that Lewis in *Mere Christianity* described as the great sin. I was also forced into the realization that my insecurities were part of a self-centered false self. For perhaps the first time in my life, I truly experienced the daily battle of dying to self that required every ounce of my spiritual will. The pain that resulted from my false sense of pride helped me finally to realize that my false self would always lead me to heartache.

Of course, in retrospect I see clearly that the pain had enabled me to recognize the importance of letting Christ the Iconoclast destroy those false pictures of self that I had allowed to be built up through my insecurities. And while those insecurities of my false self still rear their ugly heads all too frequently, I have learned through Lewis that the Creator of all has a self for me that will bring me true joy. The experiences I have described proved to be among the most painful in my life, but they were also instrumental in helping me to understand and live out the powerful insights Lewis provided about the true self. Even to this very day, the moment that I become conscious of stirrings of a feeling of self-importance, I rush directly to book 3, chapter 8 of *Mere Christianity* for my fix of reality therapy.

Mary DeKonty Applegate is professor of education at St. Joseph's University in Philadelphia, Pennsylvania. Her distinguished career as an educator has included recognition as Pennsylvania's 1993 Teacher Educator of the Year by the Pennsylvania Association of College and Teacher Educators and by the Lindback Award for Distinguished Teaching in 1983. She is the author of numerous articles in a wide range of professional journals and coauthor of *The Critical Reading Inventory*.

4

Depths That I Had Never Even Dreamed

Tony Applegate

I was raised a Catholic and attended Catholic elementary and high schools, where I was a moderately gifted but rather desultory student. At the end of my high school studies, my path was quite clearly marked: I would attend a local college, study business administration, and make my fortune. But I began to have strangely recurring thoughts about God and his insistent message that I should be doing something for others, not merely myself. It soon became apparent to me that these ideas were not about to leave of their own accord, and even my best efforts could not succeed in eliminating them altogether. Much to the surprise of my family, I decided to enter the seminary to see if this life of service was meant for me. Soon I began to experience peace and a sense of the presence of God that convinced me that I had indeed made the right choice.

The intellectual freedom I found as I pursued my studies exhilarated me. I began to read voraciously in philosophy, theology, and the history of ideas. I was acutely aware of the fact that I had no worries about where my next meal would come from or how well I was performing on my job. I came to believe firmly that the people who supported my intellectual pursuits needed people like me who could explain clearly the subtleties and philosophical nuances of the Christian faith, particularly since they had so little time in their own lives to pursue such studies. I came to believe that I had the intellectual equipment and temperament to fit the bill and to lead people to God through the path of rigorous intellectual pursuits. I discovered and devoured *Mere Christianity* but emerged from the experience virtually untouched.

In the midst of my intellectual engagement, I lost the internal peace and sense of God that had attracted me to the religious life in the first place. I missed that peace acutely and spent countless hours in prayer, trying to recover it. I began to feel, as Lewis did after the death of his wife, Joy, that God had slammed the door on me and double-bolted the lock.

After nearly seven years, I left the seminary, largely disillusioned with the church but still clinging to the belief that a person needed only his or her mind and will to pursue faith successfully and to achieve inner peace. It would be many years before I would realize that, for most of my life, I wanted God on my own terms and that I was unwilling to accept him under any other conditions.

At the age of thirty-nine, I suffered a massive heart attack, which very nearly took my life. One of my most vivid memories of that event was the forty-five minutes I spent resting alone in the intensive care unit, calculating my odds of survival. By any measure, I determined that I was more likely to die than to survive, and I knew that I should use the time to prepare myself to come before my Creator. I literally envisioned myself standing before God, eloquently presenting my case (while he, of course, listened with rapt attention) that I was not nearly as bad as the rest of humanity and that I had, comparatively speaking, earned my ticket to eternal life. I still look back on that time with a mixture of amusement and horror at my astonishing level of spiritual naïveté.

Much to the surprise of my doctors, I survived my experience almost unscathed. My heart was damaged but was functioning perfectly, and I had no symptoms of heart disease and no restrictions on my life. Unfortunately, my mind was unscathed as well, and I blithely resumed my old habits of knocking occasionally on the bolted door and congratulating myself for never having abandoned my search for God.

When my wife, Mary, approached me about increasing our spiritual commitment, I readily acceded. I expected that I would again knock on the door but would again receive no answer. But I got something very different instead. I discovered Lewis's notion of God as the hunter, "pulling at the other end of the cord," calling me to acknowledge how wrong I had been nearly all of my life. This time I was really ready to read *Mere Christianity*. As I did, I began to appreciate the fact that Lewis had dived into the nature of the Christian faith to depths that I had never even dreamed of. Perhaps Lewis's greatest gift to me is the realization that I was powerless to find my God through my fatally flawed intellect. Rather, he had been seeking me out all along.

And so I started over. Since our first forays into the world of C. S. Lewis, we have initiated a weekly C. S. Lewis adult study group and have watched with more than a little delight as his works have brought the same thrill of learning to many others. And every morning Mary and I start our day with readings from the works of our teacher. We never fail to give thanks that we encountered C. S. Lewis and welcomed into our lives his profound ideas, his inspiring faith, and the Creator who filled him (and now us) with awe. Every morning we resolve to pick ourselves up and try again despite our failures and to obey God's Word and his inspiration. And when I have the good sense not to drive them away with my pursuits of nonsense, the peace and the sense of his presence have returned to my life. I know that when my time comes to pass through the door of this life and come before my God, I won't be standing before him.

I'll be flat on my face and in complete awe. Right where I belong.

Tony Applegate is a professor of education at Holy Family University in Philadelphia, Pennsylvania. He is also a Lindback Award winner for distinguished college teaching, serves on the editorial boards of several professional publications, and is a coauthor of *The Critical Reading Inventory*.

5

An Imagination Strangely Warmed

Tom Arthur

A young college student sits in an auditorium listening to the hymn "It Is Well with My Soul," weeping as his faith slips away, for it is no longer well with his soul. A young man sits in a boardroom surrounded by other church leaders and community members as he leads them to create what will become an extremely successful community-wide C. S. Lewis festival. These are both snapshots of the same man. These are both snapshots of me. But how did I move from a loss of faith to working at a church and founding the Northern Michigan C. S. Lewis Festival? The end is also the means, and both are the works of C. S. Lewis.

In 1993 I graduated from high school and headed off to Wheaton College, a small liberal arts college outside of Chicago known both for its faith and academic commitments. Like many students at Wheaton, I was sincerely and faithfully committed to Jesus Christ. I had grown up in a Christian home and had attended church my entire life. But in my senior year of high school our youth minister was asked to leave the church for raising too many questions in the minds of young people and for not giving enough solid answers. One of those questions that lingered in the back of my mind was the question of Christianity's exclusive claims, what is often called the scandal of particularity. It is the question of our day that strikes closest to the core of Christianity. Is Jesus *the* way or *one* way among many? I could not answer this question without first answering what I thought about Jesus, and specifically, what I thought about Christianity's claim that Jesus had been raised from the dead. The pursuit of an answer to this question led me down many roads that seemed to rarely if ever have any end. I eventually realized that I was adrift. I no longer knew whether Jesus was raised from the dead, and therefore, I no longer knew whether he was the Son of God. And if he was not the Son of God, I did not know whether I could trust him above any other who ever has walked this earth or will walk this earth.

As the darkness of this drifting settled upon me, I was required to go to an orchestra concert for a music appreciation class. I figured that I would be in and out with few complications to finishing this assignment. But toward the end of the concert on the heels of a very chaotic piece, the orchestra played a version of "It Is Well." The hymn was meant to provide a sense of security after the chaos of the preceding composition. But instead of providing me with peace, the hymn seemed to amplify the chaos of the earlier piece. I broke down weeping, then sobbing, trying to hide my face from those who sat around me, embarrassed by the outward display of the state of my inward reality. At this moment I looked at life without any faith commitments and saw a dark, meaningless, and hopeless existence. My faith was gone.

The following summer my girlfriend, who would eventually become my wife, suggested that I read through C. S. Lewis's Chronicles of Narnia. I had been extremely honest with her about the state of my soul, and she thought Lewis's works might be meaningful to me. I remembered *The Lion, the Witch and the Wardrobe* having been read to me in fifth grade. Because I had enjoyed it then, I picked the books up from the local library and dove in. Soon I was engrossed. I was mostly captured by the story, but every once in a while I was surprised by the spiritual themes and theological framework that held the stories together and that gave the stories a deep meaning. It was not until I got to *The Silver Chair* that something profound happened. While reading Puddleglum's response to the Queen of Underland as she attempted to seduce Jill, Eustace, Prince Rilian, and Puddleglum into thinking that the underworld was all that existed, C. S. Lewis opened a window on my mind for God's grace to shine through and strangely warm my imagination. Puddleglum says to the witch:

> Suppose we *have* only dreamed, or made up, all those things—trees and grass and sun and moon and stars and Aslan himself. Suppose we have. Then all I can say is that, in that case, the made-up things seem a good deal more important than the real ones. . . . I'm on Aslan's side even if there isn't any Aslan to lead it. I'm going to live as like a Narnian as I can even if there isn't any Narnia. . . . Not that our lives will be very long, I should think; but that's a small loss if the world's as dull a place as you say.

Puddleglum's response gave my imagination a new answer to the questions I had been wrestling with. Puddleglum seemed to be saying that a world without meaning and hope is a world not worth believing in. Put more starkly, Puddleglum was saying that if truth is meaningless, then what is false is the better bet (of course, in a world where truth is meaningless, there really is no measure for what *is* false, and in Puddleglum's world Narnia and Aslan really are true).

At this point I made a graced-decision to put my faith back in Jesus Christ. I found that life without a commitment to him was meaningless and hopeless. It offered me no hope that I could be a better person, no hope that this world could be a better world, and no hope that there was some good and meaningful existence after death.

I say "graced-decision" only with the clarity of hindsight. At the time it felt that I was walking all alone, that *I* was making the decision. But with time behind me to reflect upon the event, I see that Lewis and Puddleglum were a means of God's grace at work in my life. As I read *The Silver Chair*, I encountered the presence of the living God, and one does not come into the presence of God and walk away unchanged. God was pursuing me through the works of Lewis long before I was ever pursuing God. As Aslan says to Jill earlier in the story, "You would not have called to me unless I had been calling to you." From this point on I began slowly to read more of Lewis's works. His nonfiction was often too much for me; I could not swallow it. But I delighted in his fiction.

Several years later I was working full-time as the Director of Ministries at Petoskey United Methodist Church and was participating in the local ministerial association. The group received a request from a local film producer to show his documentary on C. S. Lewis, *The Magic Never Ends*, to our churches. We joined together one day to watch the film and were impressed by the storyline. I had particular interest in the film because of Lewis's influence on my own faith. What eventually came out of that meeting was a month-long festival that involved over fourteen different community groups putting on over twenty events that were attended by over two thousand people. All of this took place in a town with a population of seven thousand. The festival continues annually (www.cslewisfestival.org).

When I moved on from leading the festival to attending seminary at Duke Divinity School, Lewis's influence on my life did not end. In fact, the festival had sparked in my mind another idea. During one of the festival's weekend seminars, Chris Mitchell, the director of the Marion E. Wade Center at Wheaton College (and an adviser to the festival), spoke about Lewis's participation in the Socratic Club at Oxford University. This was a place where Lewis did a considerable amount of public debating. The issues of the day tended to focus on the question of atheism and the supernatural. While today's questions are of quite a different nature (the spiritual and supernatural seem to be a commonly held belief among most postmoderns), having a group that gets together regularly to debate and discuss various ideas and issues is as much needed now as it was in Lewis's time. And so the Duke Socratic Club was born.

Lewis has not been the only influence on my faith journey with Christ, but his children's stories came along at a key moment in my life (possibly the lowest point in my spiritual life) to be a means of God's grace in my mind and, probably even more importantly, in my imagination. Lewis gave me—by means of a story and through the lips of a fictional Marshwiggle—a new solution to questions that I had been struggling with for years. The change that took place in me was clear and distinct. My faith was alive again, but there was more to do. My mind and imagination were strangely warmed.

Tom Arthur, a founder of the C. S. Lewis Festival in Petoskey, Michigan, and the Socratic Club at Duke University, is currently a seminary student at Duke Divinity School. He lives in Durham, North Carolina, with his wife, Sarah, the best-selling author of *Walking through the Wardrobe: A Devotional Quest into* The Lion, the Witch and the Wardrobe; *Walking with Frodo: A Devotional Journey through* The Lord of the Rings; and other titles.

6

Why Lewis Feels like a Friend

Anne Atkins

When asked about my first experience of C. S. Lewis, I have no love at first sight to report, no early account of his turning my life around, no gripping tale of a dark night of the soul when I picked up one of his essays and suddenly knew that I could keep going.

Then why do I love him so? Why does he feel like the tutor at my elbow telling me not to fear? When I get to heaven, the first thing I'll do is look for a cozy English pub with a crackling fire, and there in the corner I'll expect to see a figure (arguing no doubt) dressed in tatty corduroys and an old tweed sports jacket with leather patches at the elbows. Perhaps he'll still have a bit of English mud on his walking boots and a pipe churning out smoke that filters its way through the window. I will make a beeline for this scruffy figure and say, "Jack—I'm so sorry, Professor Lewis, you don't know me. But there's *so much* I want to ask you. Can I buy you another pint?"

Will he stare at me, affronted at my bad manners? Will he be annoyed at my interruption because I'm a woman? I don't know. But I do know that I have looked forward to that meeting far more than with, say, the distant figure of the great Paul of Tarsus, or the irascible and rather imposing John Milton, or the erudite Isaac Newton, or the passionate Martin Luther. It is absurdly presumptuous I know, but unlike these giants, C. S. Lewis feels like my friend. But why?

It's partly his honesty—like plunging into a mountain lake on a hot, sweaty day. Other Christians seem to present life as they think it ought to be; Lewis presents it as it is. A gracious, godly friend astonished me recently by saying he regretted that Lewis had written *A Grief Observed*, I suppose because he thought it presented a negative picture of bereavement: a Christian ought to be able to rise above such shameful bitterness. But the world I live in has pain and anger and untidy emotions that don't look good in the harsh daylight. Nevertheless, those are the emotions I feel, and Lewis's grief—the raw, brutal, and exquisitely accurately observed truth of it—has been balm to my bruised soul when I've felt the wrong emotions, too. He gives me courage to observe the world as it is, with all the wrong smells and unexpected feelings and surprising details, because this is the world God has given to us, and it is the only one worth writing about.

It's partly his clarity—like a stretching view at the end of a long climb. He never talks above my head or uses words that are too long for me (though when he writes in Greek, I sometimes need a bit of help). He uses images I understand, such as a country walk in a brisk wind. He has done that humble thing which the greatest writers do and the lesser ones neglect: he has done the work for me. He has gone to the trouble of making his ideas accessible and simple and as clear as a summer sky. He makes the life of the reader easy by allowing the life of the writer to be industrious. He prompts me to ask myself, when I'm in doubt about what I've written, *If I'd gotten up at seven to dress and feed the children, and been in the office all day, and fallen into a full tube at Victoria and had nowhere to sit, and was reading my own writing while hanging by my arm as I was jostled to and fro, would I still be able to understand what I've just written without reading the paragraph again?* If the answer is yes, I have succeeded in emulating my model.

It's also his courage that makes me consider Lewis a friend—like facing a raging storm at sea. He broadcast what many people hated to hear. He was passed over for promotion. He was misunderstood in his private life. He was loathed in his own city of Oxford (many say he still is) and only found acceptance at last in the gentler and more open-minded Cambridge. Still, he kept going. And for those of us trying to live a Christian life after him, in what is perhaps an even more hostile environment, his perseverance before us is like the rousing sound of the horn on a hair-raising day out hunting.

But most of all, he loved this world—in the way that Our Lord did. He loved the swirl of the autumn leaves, the laughter of a river, the warmth of a good drink. He knew that heaven was all this and more, and the reason he could describe the future so well was because he loved the best of the present. And how he loved! And this is what I love about him: his passion for children, the woman he adored, the entire celebration of life that God made for us to enjoy.

And that's why I want to seek him out the moment I get to the other shore. Perhaps all the intellectual questions I think I want to ask him are simply an excuse. Perhaps the overriding reason I want to find him is because, knowing him to be an Irishman at heart, I know that where Jack Lewis is, that's where the warmth and the beer and the good talk deep into the night will be.

Actress, author, broadcaster, and vicar's wife, **Anne Atkins** has always worked, despite having five children. Her latest book, *Child Rearing for Fun*, celebrates working mothers and the joy of spending time with one's children. Anne studied English at Oxford, where she currently lives with her active family, attends St. Andrew's Church, and writes. She is perhaps most widely known for her Thought for the Day commentaries on the BBC.

7

Joy Did Not Come Easily

Daniel Bailey

As a child I was given the entire set of the Chronicles of Narnia, but I read only two and a half volumes. I stopped halfway through *The Voyage of the Dawn Treader*, finding myself uninterested in imaginative tales. Over a decade later, in August 1997, during a brief church retreat along Lake Michigan's shores, a pastor recommended C. S. Lewis to me, particularly his Space Trilogy. My appearance said much that my voice did not; I had been battling depression for at least six months. I returned to the university that fall with the beginnings of an improved state of mind, as well as with the intention of learning about the things of God. Through the guidance of the Holy Spirit, I grew over the ensuing years, and C. S. Lewis—joined often by his mentor, George MacDonald, whose *Phantastes* captured my youthful passion, as well as my frustration in sorting out life, love, and belief—was alongside for the duration.

Devouring *Perelandra* in my dorm room, I remember thinking that there was no place I would rather visit. The paradise of sumptuous fruits, peculiar animals, and resplendent islands was attractive, but what truly captivated me was the innocence. Lewis portrayed the planet without sin as well as anyone (at least since Milton), and it stirred in me a longing that I soon came to identify as hunger for God, for that most intimate of relationships. I had long believed in God and had been a Christian (though at times nominally so) for some years, but what I was reading in the Bible that fall and what God was impressing on my heart was that I had terribly underestimated the significance of faith. On Perelandra (Venus to us) God's presence was everywhere, pervading everything and everyone. Our earth (Thulcandra in the trilogy) has not recognized this for a very long time. I found myself crying out for that lost love. I had inwardly affirmed and publicly acknowledged a set of religious beliefs, but I did not know real worship. Imagining the planet of perfection certainly made my own sinful nature clear to me, but I was too enamored with the atmosphere of redemption to remain mired in condemnation. Lewis showed me with his words that he knew vital salvation, and he impressed upon me a concrete longing for it.

Joy does not always come easily, especially during depression, but in reading *Perelandra* I learned the blessing of fighting for it. Throughout the Space Trilogy, the protagonist Elwin Ransom grapples with his role in multiple worlds. On Perelandra, Ransom experiences depression in addition to isolation, confusion, apprehension, and skepticism. While externally he is caught up in a cosmic struggle between heaven and hell, internally he is engaged in a struggle more enervating than anything he experienced on earth. I have always liked how Lewis portrays Ransom as fighting the devilish Un-man with his mind *and* his body, because sometimes it takes every sort of strength to fight for good—especially in the midst of depression. Ransom the man is taken beyond the earth, but his spirit travels beyond the known universe; he returns to earth a champion, far more healthful and youthful than when he left. His character helped me see the value in continuing to fight depression by refusing to serve it. God had a specific task for Ransom, and Ransom is committed to doing it, despite what he regards as his limitations. My own desire for joy was alien to me during my darkest hours, but the fierce truth and beauty of Lewis's imagery helped me receive it.

Lewis further mentored me regarding the duty of servanthood. That fall I knew very little about C. S. Lewis's life, but I felt closer to him than I ever had to other authors. I didn't know until years later the familial tragedies Lewis experienced in childhood or the actual and intellectual wars of his early adulthood. When I eventually read *Surprised by Joy*, I discovered the same honest, approachable Lewis whom I had met unexpectedly in *Perelandra*. From Ransom's plunging into an unknown ocean and learning to walk anew, to his maturing and ultimately praising God in the Great Dance, *Perelandra* suggests a journey from birth to death and even to resurrection. Knowing the specific trials Lewis experienced gave me a realistic perspective of my life before God—that no matter what happens to me, I am not alone, and depression cannot deny God's purpose. Although *The Pilgrim's Regress* is the most autobiographical of Lewis's fictional works, I believe that Lewis conveys his thoughts and feelings about life in every one of his books. It was not Lewis's vibrant imagination or his acute intellect, but rather his appreciation of the deepest truths of the human condition—the triumphs and the tragedies—that was most important to me. He *knew* what he wrote. He didn't just think of it; he lived it. We all have our secrets, but Lewis is one of the most appropriately transparent writers I have ever read. As illustrated in Ransom's journey, Lewis helped reveal to me how we all stand bare before God.

One devastating effect of depression is an apparent divide between the mind and the heart. Thoughts and emotions become clouded and often disconnected, sometimes severely. We have been created, however, as both intellectual and sensual beings. Lewis's writings showed me that to be fully human and Christian, the mind and the heart cannot be separated. Approaching God with one or the other, we lose half of the relationship. A life without both is empty and miserable. I have always been an intellectual. My challenge has been the sensual, allowing myself to experience pleasure and accepting enjoyment unburdened by analysis. Ransom's narration, for example, reflects both pure delight in and elaborate study of the flora and fauna of Perelandra. I might have easily overindulged in the latter. Lewis modeled for me how living in the light of God's presence means stimulating emotion, not suppressing it or permitting it to be suppressed. Lewis communicated to me the joys that await a mind and heart fully united.

In publishing fine secular as well as Christian books, Lewis also showed me that faith and reason serve best and shine brightest when they are bound together. Surrendering one for the sake of the other causes both to wither. In my field, I am encountering new horizons in nanotechnology, which involves building and characterizing materials and devices at the nanoscale, or atomic level. (A nanometer is one *billionth* of a meter, about one *ten-thousandth* the width of a human hair.) Work at the nanoscale will revolutionize energy, computers, medicine, and security. I am fortunate that my reason never abolished my faith; I witness no conflict between God and science. Yet I have lived this duality largely in private. Lewis modeled how to live both publicly. There is a cost. Just as Ransom's heel, bitten by the Un-man, never fully heals, Lewis was denied a full professorship for many years, likely because of his spiritual sentiments and popularity. My academic life, focused on novel photovoltaic cell design, is far removed from Lewis's specialty, English literature. Yet as a Christian, my ultimate goal in chemistry is in some small way to do with molecules what I see that Lewis did with words—to co-create with God in a way that ultimately honors God and blesses his children. Lewis has helped me recognize that the church needs Christian men and women in the secular academy who neither subvert nor flaunt their faith, but who work hard in their chosen calling, representing Jesus Christ in doing things well.

I appreciate Lewis's logical arguments and his remarkable imagery, but his greatest legacy to me has been his gift of speaking as a friend, sharing his joys and sorrows. A pervasive theme in his writings—and perhaps the best compliment I could give Lewis as a man—is consistency. He lived consistently for God and exalted God consistently in word and deed.

Daniel Bailey earned a Bachelor of Science degree from the University of Illinois at Urbana-Champaign in 2004. In addition to contributing articles to *Analytical Chemistry* and the *Journal of Agricultural and Food Chemistry*, he writes poetry and essays, with several of the latter appearing in *Salt*, a Christian magazine. He also enjoys tennis and volleyball and has performed in several humorous musicals. A bibliophile, he has more books than he can possibly read, but he would like to add to them by attempting to write fiction. Currently living in Evanston, Illinois, Bailey plans to complete his Ph.D. in materials chemistry in 2009.

8

I Became a Believer

Eddy Benmuvhar

I was born in Istanbul to Jewish parents. My ancestors had moved to Turkey after the Jews were expelled from Spain during the Spanish Inquisition in the fifteenth century. I came to the United States as a young man to study engineering in New York City. There I met my wife, Rosemarie. She came from a non-practicing mixed marriage (Christian and Jewish), and for the first ten years of our marriage we gave little thought to our spiritual life.

I was busy traveling the world as a civil engineer. As project manager for a large consulting firm in New York, I was put in charge of highway and dam construction projects in a variety of countries. After New York, I took the family to Spain for five years, where I served as project director for several U.S. military installations.

A turning point in our lives came when we moved to New Jersey, next door to a friendly Christian couple, Nils and Marjorie Westerberg, who handed me the book *Mere Christianity*. I set it aside as I did most other writings on religion; it did not seem relevant to my lifestyle and my agnostic beliefs. My wife, however, came to know the Lord through this couple.

Almost thirty years later, through life experiences and the love and faithfulness of my Christian wife, I began to give more serious thought to the state of my spiritual poverty. I began reading the Bible and then picked up that C. S. Lewis book given to me years earlier by those New Jersey neighbors. In *Mere Christianity* I found a clear explanation of the existence of God. Lewis made the reality of the gospel compelling and persuasive. He did not delve into theological intricacies that might bog down the simple message of my needing salvation and redemption. God used the writings of C. S. Lewis as well as the strong faith demonstrated by the saved people around me to bring me to himself.

It was at home on a quiet afternoon when I felt God's Spirit enter into my heart. On September 5, 1996, at age seventy-two, I became a believer in Jesus Christ as the promised Messiah and as my personal Savior. I began to understand all the things I could not comprehend before—the reality of God, the validity of the Bible, the prophecies of the Old Testament, and their fulfillment in Jesus in the New Testament. I look at life and death differently now. Quoting the Apostle Paul, "I am not ashamed of the gospel of Christ, for it is the power of God to salvation for everyone who believes, for the Jew first and also for the Greek" (Rom. 1:16 NKJV). I shared this wonderful moment with my wife, and now with you. The Lord gave us two wonderful years together before Rosemarie died of leukemia in 1998.

Eddy Benmuvhar is a retired civil engineer living in Palm Beach, Florida. A graduate of Robert College, Istanbul, and the University of Illinois (M.A. in civil engineering), Mr. Benmuvhar is fluent in English, French, Spanish, and Turkish. He volunteers with the AARP Free Tax Organization, belongs to a Presbyterian church, and enjoys his life by the seaside, helping others.

9

An Alluring Sense of Wonder

Ronald W. Bresland

I was around seven years old when I first encountered the writings of C. S. Lewis. The story which had made the strongest impression on me up to that point, *Old Yeller* by Fred Gipson, was soon displaced by my discovery of Lewis's novel *The Lion, the Witch and the Wardrobe*. There is an incident in Lewis's story when Lucy, while playing a game of hide-and-seek in Professor Kirk's house, hides in an old wardrobe only to find, as she fumbles about in the darkness, that she has stumbled on an entrance into Narnia. I can still vividly recall my own experience of hearing this as a child: the hushed expectation of a dozen wide-eyed schoolchildren sitting cross-legged in the corner of a small classroom in County Tyrone, listening intently while our teacher led us through the wardrobe door, past the fur coats, and—snow crunching gently underfoot—into another world. I suspect my own imaginative life started at that point. I have found that this incident in the story has proved to be an equally profound moment for many others—the sudden realization that the possibility exists for an *other world*, a world far removed from our everyday experience.

As a young boy growing up in rural Northern Ireland, I was captivated by the very idea that I could step out of my world into the unknown. I was as much at home in the fictional Texas world of Birdsong Creek as I was in Narnia. The way of life in the Texas countryside during the mid-1800s depicted in *Old Yeller* was not too removed from my own early life of tending crops, raising animals, hunting, shooting, and fishing. Likewise, the Narnian landscape seemed familiar; its hills, streams, and lakes were not essentially different from those in my experience. When I read Lewis's vivid descriptions of the Narnian countryside studded with its hawthorn and gorse bushes, I had only to look out my window to recognize the surroundings. In reading the Narnian stories I was captivated, not so much by the environment of Narnia or the realization that Lewis was a fellow Ulsterman, but by the unsettling and alluring sense of wonder and desire that these stories evoked within me. That such a place could in some way reflect a person's desire for heaven did not occur to me then, but for Lewis—as I would later discover—this desire for heaven informed all genres of his work and motivated many of his writings.

From such dimly realized intimations as this, my love of story would eventually lead me to earn degrees in English and Anglo-Irish literature. The interim period between my first childhood taste of Lewis and my later academic engagement with his work was punctuated only by a brief encounter with his Space Trilogy, when my interest in the science fiction genre was at its height, driven by writers such as Robert Sheckley and Philip José Farmer. It was not until 1997, when I was engaged by the C. S. Lewis Centenary Group in Northern Ireland to research aspects of Lewis's Irish background, that I fully grasped the extent of that influence on his imagination. Now, over a decade later, that influence becomes more apparent as my understanding of Lewis deepens.

This sustained period of engagement with Lewis's writings has undoubtedly had a significant impact on my spiritual life. When I set out on the serious study of his work, I was not a Christian; now, a number of years later, I am. I then had a denomination but no knowledge of Jesus Christ as my personal Savior; now I have both. C. S. Lewis was among those factors that helped shape my thought, and that eventually brought me to Christ. It is only now when I look back on how people, situations, and influences were used in my conversion that I see the guiding and gracious hand of the Holy Spirit at work in my life. I had managed for over forty years, or so I thought, to keep God at bay. Since my adolescence, the Lord's admonition to the Laodiceans, "because thou art lukewarm, and neither cold nor hot, I will spew thee out of my mouth," (Rev. 3:16 ASV) had fixed itself in my mind as the standard I would ultimately have to meet.

I was challenged by the writings of Lewis to confront what, if anything, I actually did believe. Lewis's readiness to address the fundamental questions of Christian belief—coupled with his robust, intellectual arguments in defense of Christianity—appealed to my head and my heart; I found his reputation as an "apostle to the skeptics" entirely justified. Lewis's ability to present complex moral arguments in everyday language and his observation that if you can't turn your faith into the vernacular, "then either you don't understand it or you don't believe it," made an indelible impression on me.

My debt to Lewis is great. His writings have enlightened and enriched my spiritual understanding and have been incalculably valuable (to paraphrase Lewis) as a pointer to something other and outer. In the closing pages of his autobiography, *Surprised by Joy*, I find particularly resonant the vivid analogy of travelers who are lost in the woods. The sudden discovery of a signpost initially excites enthusiasm and relief among the wayfarers, but its relevance becomes less significant once they are on the right road and are passing signposts every few miles. Such is the influence of our spiritual mentors. We are grateful for the reassurance they provide, but having found ourselves on the right road, we follow where it leads. Like C. S. Lewis—"We would be at Jerusalem."

Ronald W. Bresland is one of the leading authorities on C. S. Lewis's Irish life and background. He was formerly a Cultural Traditions Fellow of the Institute of Irish Studies, The Queen's University of Belfast (1997–1998). His book *The Backward Glance: C. S. Lewis and Ireland* (1999) explored the many connections between Lewis and Ireland. He has lectured and contributed to documentaries on Lewis in the United Kingdom and the United States. His latest work, *Travel with C. S. Lewis*, was published by DayOne Publications in 2006. Visit the author's website at www.cslewisinireland.com.

10

Coming In Out of the Wind

Jill Briscoe

It was in Britain in the fifties after the Second World War, and I was training to be a teacher at a college in Cambridge. This august place of learning was exciting, heady, and very stretching. People believed all sorts of things about all sorts of things, and some had chosen to believe nothing at all about nothing at all! They debated the merits of such in the pubs, on the banks of the Cam River, in the ancient halls of learning, and in the dorms. I reveled in it all.

Some learned theologian in Germany had decided that God was dead, and we self-conscious, clever, and erudite students seriously considered this interesting possibility. I wondered who had acquired such complete knowledge to come to this stupendous conclusion. Surely only someone who knew everything there was to know could announce the death of the Almighty.

Then Christmas came, my first at Cambridge. Our noisy and rather arrogant group of girls obeyed tradition and went together to King's College chapel for the famous Christmas Eve service. We marveled at the building's spectacular architecture and the old-fashioned music. We observed what was (to us) the misplaced congregational reverence for all things holy in such a day and age. Sitting in an ancient pew and looking at the ancient vicar to match, we wondered how long the ancient service would last. I took note of the incredibly ancient Bible that was chained to the lectern for safety. "Quite right," I muttered to the equally skeptical friend at my side, "that's exactly where that book belongs, chained to the past!"

My mind wandered to stories I had heard growing up in the British school system when our Scripture teacher had taught us the Bible. It was a good Church of England curriculum, so I still remembered the rudiments of the dogmas of the Christian faith. I remembered the doctrines of creation and the fall, redemption and glory. The concepts of heaven and hell had seemed plausible back then. But that was in grade school. Hitler had dominated my life for years, and somehow hell was believable because of the concentration camps and the ghoulish things people were enduring on our broken globe. As C. S. Lewis would later write in *The Problem of Pain*, "There is no doctrine which I would more willingly remove from Christianity than this (the doctrine of Hell), if it lay in my power. But it has the full support of Scripture and, specially, of Our Lord's own words; it has always been held by Christendom; and it has the proper support of reason. If a game is played, it must be possible to lose it."

I later learned that Lewis handled the doctrines of heaven and hell with great skill, sending both into the battle over the prevailing disbelief in the supernatural. Out of all his books, the powerful imagery in *The Great Divorce* later gave me an unforgettable picture of the ominous emptiness of the Grey Town. Totally self-centered folk departed after death to the Grey Town, where they were haunted by the fear that the grey would someday turn into infinite night. There is no hope of escaping the Grey Town, which houses real personalities who have absolutely no meaning or significance.

Just as Lewis brought hell into the war against unbelief, so he brought heaven to the front lines of the battle. It was *The Weight of Glory* that later made heaven believable for me. And not only believable, but also attainable through the Christ who was the love of Lewis's life after years spent as a formidable antagonist to all things Christian. He writes, "At present we are on the outside of the world, the wrong side of the door. . . . We cannot mingle with the splendours we see. But all the leaves of the New Testament are rustling with the rumour that it will not always be so. Some day, God willing, we shall get *in*." And again: "A cleft has opened in the pitiless walls of the world, and we are invited to follow our great Captain inside." GLORY!

I read Lewis's brilliant perceptions of heaven and hell some time later. But in the meantime, it was not difficult for me to acknowledge the very real possibility of hell. The evidence of people behaving hellishly had become overwhelmingly evident as the Allies liberated the Nazi concentration camps. It was easy to conceive of another evil realm, a place where hellish things happened in an afterworld. Reason also dictated that there must be an opposite to this hellishness. So it was that I came to believe in the "reasonableness" of hell. As I tried to make sense of it all, I was amazed to find that heaven was the breathless hope of my heart! Surely there was a saving "opposite" of the atrocious living nightmare we had endured during the war. Glory was a distinct, obvious necessity for hope to be realized, or all was lost and life truly was meaningless.

If, at this time, I had read Lewis's famous words in *Mere Christianity*, "If I find in myself a desire which no experience in this world can satisfy, the most probable explanation is that I was made for another world," perhaps I would have sought a little more diligently to test his theory for myself. But other things crowded out my more introspective moments. Things I had believed in the past gave way to things I believed in the present.

The present was postwar Britain—a country decimated by the worldwide conflict that had been raging for too many years. A Britain that had gone to church before the war but that did not return after the war. The war was a recent, horrible memory; I was a teenager, churchless and increasingly godless, fumbling around for a reason to be significant and staggering toward truth.

At Cambridge truth was up for grabs; ancient belief systems such as Christianity were dismantled. There were so many clever people who were apparently living complete lives and who seemed to do very well without any spiritual dimension to their thinking. It was only the dumber variety of student, I decided, who appeared to gravitate toward a form of Christianity that caused them to be obnoxious and insistent on being listened to. Or was it? I found myself taking a closer look.

I was playing tennis for my college, and I discovered to my chagrin that the captain of the tennis team was "one of them." My debating captain (a bright and beautiful girl from Northern Ireland) was one of them, too.

At that time, in the world of Cambridge lived this man C. S. Lewis. He was professor of medieval and Renaissance English, though just then I had no awareness of his burgeoning influence. If only I had known he would become one of the most important Christian thinkers and writers of our century! His famous book *The Screwtape Letters* was republished during those years. I could not have known that this very book would be the first Christian book that I would read.

Life at school continued on apace, and I enjoyed it all. Yet a nagging sense of unease persisted. Despite all my efforts, my thoughts would wander. I would be irritated with the cheerful way our tennis captain lost a match! Her good sportsmanship rebuked bad sportsmanship. I knew her attitude had something to do with her faith. And then one night I got really sick, and the school rushed me to the hospital.

In the next few days as my condition worsened, I had nothing to do but revisit the stirring of my soul and, without words, cry out to a God I wasn't even sure existed. He had, of course, everything lined up to answer that heart cry. In a ward of some twenty people, a Christian was in the bed next to mine. Janet was a nurse who herself was sick, but though in pain was alert enough to take me on as a project!

It didn't take her and God long. A few short glorious days of unpacking the truth and feeding it to me in bite-sized pieces convinced me. This was truth that I wonderingly believed. This was about Jesus. This was about what my sin did to him. This was about his everlasting love demonstrated in a manger, on a cross, and in an empty tomb. Suddenly I was back in my bomb shelter as a little girl, no longer wondering about the validity of creation, the fall, redemption, and glory, but embracing it all. I cried bitter, sorry tears. For the first time in my thoroughly self-centered life, I cried for someone other than myself. I cried for him. For the cross he had to endure to bring me home.

The next day, a copy of *The Screwtape Letters* appeared on my bedside table. "Read it," Janet advised. "The devil is mad he has lost you, and you must not be ignorant of his devices." And so my spiritual education began with C. S. Lewis's startling images of the old devils and the young devils who desire to chew us up and spit us out to assuage their diabolical hunger. It began with the images from this man's pen that I have never forgotten—images that have hugely influenced my journey of faith.

Those images not only influenced my thinking and believing, but my teaching and writing, too. I think, write, and teach using images and pictures, allegory and fantasy married to fact. As most disciples do, I try to emulate my Master Teacher as I seek to awaken my world to the cornerstone doctrines of the faith—creation, fall, redemption, and glory—doctrines I believe with all my heart, soul, mind, and strength. When I get to heaven, I will most certainly ask to spend one of my first days off with C. S. Lewis.

I will thank him for his book that warned me that the devil will attack my "holy habits" first, last, and always. In his book, Uncle Screwtape reproaches the apprentice demon, Wormwood, for permitting his "patient" to become a Christian. "All the *habits* of the patient, both mental and bodily, are still in our favour."

If a convert's habits remain the same, they will realize little of their life in Christ. I credit Lewis with "frightening" me into holy habits that have lasted a lifetime. He encourages the disciple of Jesus to "keep listening to that other voice . . . [to come] in out of the wind."

It was Lewis who alerted me to the absolute necessity of stretching the sides of my soul devotionally day by daily day, and Lewis who insisted that the friend of Christ not grow weary in well doing and in the work of God. As I have practiced what Lewis calls "coming in out of the wind," God has renewed and smoothed the frayed edges of my emotions until I am refreshed and ready to do battle again. The writings of C. S. Lewis have helped me celebrate God through everyday experiences. To look for and bask in those patches of what he calls "Godlight."

I will also thank Lewis for his raw honesty and how he wrestled through his ministry with a broken heart. How hard it is for famous Christians to bear private grief publicly, and yet how wonderfully does this mighty literary giant invite us into his pain. He shares with the world his search for solid ground as he watched Joy Davidman, the love of his life, fight her death battles.

"How, C. S.," I will ask, "did you ever manage to allow your searing personal pain to drive you to God and not away from him? It is hard when you are hurting so much emotionally that you can hardly breathe to spare some special time to comfort others in similar predicaments by your honest wonderings and triumphant conclusions." I am grateful that he allowed us into those sacred places. And I will want him to know that he has helped so many of us when our own time of testing has come.

Lewis also used illustrations that relate to my world as a woman, unlike some preachers who use male illustrations only. Today in church I am surprised too seldom by an illustration that belongs to my woman's world. In *The Four Loves* Lewis uses images from a woman's world, such as kitchen implements or homemade stories, to draw us into his meanings of *agape*, *phileo*, and *eros* love. I understand and relate to his pictures and parables because he took time to understand me—a woman. He listened, observed, and has felt my "womanness" enough to use it to instruct my spirit in its quest for godliness and selfless love.

C. S. Lewis was a critic, a satirist, a visionary, and an apologist. I believe that in the New Millennium we have now moved beyond the New Modernity, which among other things took us from "thinking to feeling," and that the horrendous events of September 11, 2001, shocked us into returning from feeling to thinking again! On the infamous eleventh of September, I found myself in the air on the way from Moscow to Chicago. I ended up being diverted to Newfoundland, along with thousands of other flyers in dozens of carriers. There I was stranded for six and one-half days in a Salvation Army hall. I was surprised to discover that these were some of the most wonderful days of my life!

Not only did I have a chance to check and see if my theology was in good shape, but I had the wonderful opportunity to spend "talk time" with the 250 people on my flight who had nothing else to do but think about the issues of life and death that had suddenly and rudely interrupted our lives. In conversations that week I discovered myself drawing on my Lewis memories, concepts, and quotes. Once more it was time to face people up with his challenges. Truth, of course, is true for all times and conditions of humanity, but the approach that Lewis took to explain it to the "man on the street" was exceptionally useful during that stressful time. It was a glorious week!

For this unprecedented opportunity, as people's minds have been shocked awake, we have C. S. Lewis, in all his depth and richness—a thinker who speaks clearly to our day and age, unscrewing the inscrutable and explaining the unexplainable. The time is right, and the fields of the world are ripe for harvest. Lewis puts a sickle in our hands. We should use the tools that this master writer and thinker has left behind for us as weapons in our arsenal to make Screwtape and his devils sorry they started the whole mess in the first place!

Jill Briscoe is an internationally known speaker and author who cofounded with her husband, Stuart, Telling the Truth media ministries.

Jill is the executive editor of *Just Between Us*, a magazine for women in ministry and leadership. She is the author of more than forty books, including *Prayer That Works* and *Faith Enough to Finish*. A native of Liverpool, England, Jill resides with Stuart in suburban Milwaukee.

11

He Saved My Dying Faith

Justice Carmon

She was dead, and there was nothing I could do about it.

My life as I had known it was over, and my home was taken. I was twenty years old, and the only thing that kept me believing in the existence of God and the deity of Jesus Christ was an Oxford don named C. S. Lewis.

Lewis himself struggled with his faith in God after the death of his own mother, becoming less and less of a believer until he was fully entrenched in the campgrounds of brilliant heathens warming themselves by the fires of humanists who had gone before.

Within a year of my mother's death, I also drew near their camp, enjoying the bitter camaraderie of the wounded, neglected, and abused. We were young men full of strength, who read poetry and fantasy to salve the wounds we had incurred in a fallen world.

Dark angels demand dark minstrels, and fools had better beware. The times were not in our favor; the Moral Majority was reaching its height and Jim and Tammy Faye Bakker were in high form, proving the vacuousness of Christian thought, smothered in makeup, TV lights, and requests for money. The movie *Blade Runner* was our Bible, and

Anne Rice was our lady, her dark, iconoclastic vampire, Lestat, living life as an immortal sans deity.

Bright Christians running around with vapid slogans of God's love affected us not at all. Their pain was too small, their wounds superficial and easily sneered at. Bitter at a God who created people for us to love and then let them and our dreams die, we renounced all that was didactic, holy, reverent.

But the most amazing thing happened in the middle of this: I refused to let go of my faith that there was a God who knew all and saw everything—a God who brought his children who die into heaven to give them eternal life and joy. For that, I owe a great debt to C. S. Lewis.

I knew that Lewis's mother had died when he was young, and like all the terrifically analytical, I did not consider that losing your mother at the age of twelve was the same as losing her at the age of twenty—but the wounds are similar, especially considering that Lewis lived in a different age. We modern children have an amazingly long adolescence, thanks in large part to our entertainment and lesser responsibilities.

Lewis's main contribution to me was not that he was a brilliant and concise writer, but that he was a writer who had suffered great loss, developed a keen mind, and still placed his faith in Christ. His personal wounds enabled him to speak with tact and wisdom about the necessity of a God with a clear moral standard, a God outside space-time, and therefore Lord of all. A God who permitted pain in a fallen world to awaken us, to save us from being lulled into hell, self-satisfied and smug as our last breath escapes.

As I read *Mere Christianity* and *The Problem of Pain* at my mother's bedside, I was taught by this Oxford don. Lewis died before I was born, but Lewis made us think about the philosophical impact of Christian thought—what is now called a worldview. Why pain? Why suffering? Why Christ? Was Jesus God? What did Christianity offer that was so different from other religions?

In writing these books, Lewis was wrestling with his own theology, his own loss, I think. Thank God for that. Because he forearmed me, though I did not know it.

Lewis's argument of "Lunatic, Liar, or Lord" arrested me. I knew that Jesus claimed to be God, and either this was absolutely true or Jesus was absolutely insane. Of course, at that time I did not know Jesus in any intimate way. I argued with my atheist friends, but slowly and surely I discovered that the world was not my friend, that nonbelievers could practice utter immorality without remorse, and that, despite my waywardness, many believers were kind, truly kind. Lewis was right, but I couldn't admit how wrong I was.

What Lewis did was speak to me logically as my heart was breaking. Those times at my mother's bedside were having an effect. Lewis's words kept coming back. He didn't lie to me, he didn't hide the facts, and he didn't live or write arrogantly. He was humble in his faith, aware of pain and the need for redemption. Intuitively I knew this. Any man who will take the time to write books like he did was serious. Later, when facing the end of his life, he said, "Ten years from now no one will care what I have written."

On that, Lewis was wrong, dead wrong. His work saved my dying faith. I look forward to the day when I'll tell Jack this to his face. With Jesus.

Justice Carmon is a freelance writer, caregiver, and Bible teacher who lives in Wheaton, Illinois. He has been a housefather in the inner city of Memphis and engages in short-term mission trips to Kazakhstan, Russia, and India.

12

Like Waking Up

Greg Clarke

I'm an INTJ. The initiates know what I mean, and they draw in their breath.

Oh, they exclaim. He's willful, and he thinks he's always right. He doesn't give out, at least not in the way I need. And he's so stuck in the world of ideas that he'd rather read than talk, rather plot than party, and he'll complete a project that no one else will ever see just for the sheer satisfaction of it.

It's a personality description from the Myers-Briggs personality test, and my wife and I have found it a useful tool, especially in marriage (I'm married to a delightful and gregarious ENFJ, who says that my profile explains everything she ever suspected about me but found out too late!).

I was insulted when I came out of the test as an INTJ until I noticed that on the list of probable INTJs throughout history was one Clive Staples Lewis. I claimed the label with pride then and there—I didn't want to retake the test, in case it recategorized me somewhere else!

Lewis has been part of my life since I read *The Lion, the Witch and the Wardrobe* when I was, I think, eight. It came to me in a lovely boxed paperback set from my evangelical parents, and I still have the set. Aslan was as good a Christ figure as a young boy could hope for—powerful and kind all at once, a trustworthy leader with a sense of humor (something I've always valued) and the voice of wisdom. It was Lewis's wisdom that meant most to me as I sought to understand what it meant to be a follower of Christ.

The Magician's Nephew, more than *The Lion, the Witch and the Wardrobe*, developed my sense of otherworldliness. I expected the appearance of rambunctious queens, sudden journeys to pools in other dimensions, and an encounter with a Lion that sings things into being. It didn't seem to bother me that none of these things was in fact happening; I read them, so they occurred where it mattered—in my imagination.

Lewis's otherworldliness established for me an unshakeable contentment with unseen realities. It seems to me that the doctrines of the Christian faith require a certain capacity to imagine what might be the case beyond the confines of space and time, and for me these were simple imaginings. My mind had been prepared to receive them by the Wood between the Worlds.

Lewis's wisdom came to me in the form of aphoristic interventions in the drama of teenage doubt. I believed Christianity like the sun—not only seeing it but seeing everything by it. There were no ordinary people, just immortal horrors or everlasting splendors. The doors of hell were locked on the inside. Pain was God's megaphone to rouse a deaf world. The heart of Christianity is a myth that is also a fact.

I was reading existentialist literature, listening to the Smiths and the Cure, and watching Monty Python and Woody Allen films. But these were met by, among other things, Lewis's refreshing words. Lewis never brushed aside for me the impact of these modern forays into meaninglessness; rather, he offered both reasons and emotions that caused me to lean toward meaningfulness instead. I felt the sway in both directions, and God gave me Lewis and others to keep me leaning toward him. For that, I will always be grateful.

I read a lot of Lewis's essays as an undergraduate and keep returning to them now, discovering anew just how good they are. I admired Lewis's ability to argue relentlessly about a topic but then come to what seemed to me usually a humane and gentle conclusion. Take, for instance, his essay on Christianity and culture. For a dilettantish arts undergraduate, this essay was a swift kick in just the right place. I learned from it that Lewis shared both my love for cultural life and my iconoclastic reactions against it as a gospel-shaped, eschatologically driven Christian. How could I spend all this time reading fiction when there was a world out there that needed salvation? I learned, too, that the Bible neither elevated culture to the status of religion, nor denigrated it as worthless. The truth would be found awkwardly, humbly, somewhere in between. I learned that culture was a storehouse of sub-Christian values, often a pleasure and an inspiration, but never a salvation. I turned this into my own expression, used often now, that culture can provide epiphanies but not theophanies. Lewis would have said it better, but I owe the thought to him.

During my Ph.D. years, I had reason to visit Wheaton College in Illinois, where I was billeted by the Martindales. Wayne Martindale, a leading Lewis scholar and teacher, gave me his recently published collection of Lewis quotations, *The Quotable Lewis*. It was this work that alerted me to the fact that I quoted Lewis to myself with a kind of catechetic intent—to assuage doubts, to summarize thought clouds, to remember principles, and to spur myself on to love and good deeds. Lewis didn't replace Scripture (never fear, brothers and sisters!), but he expressed what I needed to know in a way that impressed itself upon me. Perhaps it's just that shared INTJ personality, but I suspect it is much more than that.

In Australia we have launched a conference called C. S. Lewis Today (www.cslewistoday.com). Our inaugural gathering saw around 300 people in Sydney and Melbourne celebrating, exploring, and engaging with the range of Lewis's work. At the conference two people gave their lives to Christ. It was something that we on the organizing committee had prayed for but never really expected to happen (at least I didn't). But when I heard the news, a Lewis aphorism sprang to mind immediately and captured what it is like for so many of us to come to Christ: "like when a man, after long sleep, still lying motionless in bed, becomes aware that he is now awake."

Greg Clarke is the director of the Centre for Apologetic Scholarship and Education (CASE) at New College, University of New South Wales, Sydney, and a visiting fellow in its School of English. He is the author of *Is It Worth Believing? The Spiritual Challenge of the Da Vinci Code* (Sydney: Matthias Media, 2005) and *Eschatology, Apocalypse and Modern Fiction* (forthcoming, Ashgate Press, UK). Greg and his wife, Amelia, have three children and live in Botany, Sydney's southwest side. Greg loves cricket, U2, good sketch comedy, playing bass guitar, fine dining with his wife, and not-so-fine dining with their children.

13

From Atheism to Belief

Francis S. Collins

I grew up in a home in the Shenandoah Valley of Virginia, where faith was not regularly practiced. My parents were very creative people, particularly in theater and the arts. They taught me at home until the sixth grade but not because of the desire to instill religious beliefs in me—as is now often the case in homeschooling—but just to keep me out of the hands of the country schools, whose teachers were perceived as being a little less than encouraging to the creative instincts of my mother's four boys. She inspired in me a desire to learn things. But I did not learn much about faith or gain a belief in God. I was sent to church at the age of six, for a very specific reason—to join the boys' choir in order to learn music. I remember an exhortation from my father, who said, "You're there to learn the music. There's going to be this other puzzling stuff about theology. Don't pay any attention to that. It will just confuse you." So I followed those instructions, and I learned a lot about music, but I had no clue what was going on in terms of the rest of those services.

When my friends in the dormitory at college quizzed me about what I believed, I realized I had absolutely no idea. It was fairly easy for me to decide I did not believe any of this stuff that some of the people were talking about—about Christ or other forms of religious faith. I assumed that it was all superstition. I had gotten along quite well without it and did not feel any particular need to embrace it.

I finished my undergraduate degree in chemistry and went on to work on a Ph.D. in chemical physics at Yale. After delving into that particular field and concluding that the only real truths were second-order differential equations, there seemed to be even less need for God. God did not seem to me like he would be a second-order differential equation. So I became a rather obnoxious atheist in graduate school. If you had gone to lunch with me, you would not have enjoyed the experience. I had absolutely no interest in matters of the spiritual life, because I did not think there was such a thing.

But then I changed directions. Deciding that biology was a lot more interesting than I had ever thought, I determined to go to medical school. I wanted to learn that particular discipline in order to apply my scientific instincts in a human health direction. As a medical student, I encountered many people going through terrible suffering, stricken down with diseases not of their own making. Yet, I could not help but note that some of these people appeared to have incredible faith. They were not angry with God, which I thought they should have been. If they believed in a God and he let them get cancer, why weren't they shaking their fist at him? Instead, they seemed to derive this remarkable sense of comfort from their faith, even at a time of great adversity. That response really puzzled me. A few of my patients asked what I believed; I stammered and stuttered and realized I was too embarrassed to say, "I don't know."

Then something came to me. As a scientist, I had always insisted on collecting rigorous data before drawing a conclusion. And yet, in matters of faith, I had never collected any data at all. I did not know what I had rejected. So I decided I should be a little better grounded in my atheism. I had better find out what this is all about. I challenged a patient Methodist minister down the street. After listening to my questions and realizing I was not dealing with a very full deck of information, he suggested that I read the Gospel of John, which I did. I found that Scripture to be interesting, puzzling, and not at all what I had thought faith was about. But still, I was not ready to consider the plausibility of faith; I needed more of an intellectual basis to get past my own arguments about why this was just superstition. For that purpose, he turned me to the writings of C. S. Lewis in his classic book *Mere Christianity*. (Even today, *Mere Christianity* seems to be the very best book to put in the hands of a young seeker who is trying to figure out if there is rationality for faith.) So I read *Mere Christianity*, and my materialist view was quickly laid to ruins. Particularly compelling for me was Lewis's argument about the law of human nature: Why was it there? Why is it universal? Also his argument: Would not this be the place to look for evidence of a personal, perfect, and holy God if there was one?

Sociobiologists will argue that human nature is all, in some way, an evolutionary consequence. That just never seemed particularly compelling to me as an explanation for the moral law: that we know somehow intrinsically, and yet often do not obey. Here is a wonderful sentence from *Mere Christianity*: "We find out more about God from the moral law than from the universe in general, just as you find out more about a man by listening to his conversation than by looking at a house he has built." I realized that my scientific life was looking at the house, while I had never considered the conversation (the moral law) as evidence of God. I needed to study the Creator. After struggling many months, I realized that if there was a God, he was holy and I was not. I realized for the first time just how flawed a person I was. I then recognized what Christ did by providing a bridge between God and all his holiness and me and all my unholiness. Finally I gave in and surrendered—not perhaps, like Lewis, the most dejected and reluctant convert in all England, which is how he described his conversion. A rush of warm emotion did certainly not afflict me either. Rather, it was very much like walking into a complete unknown. God is good, and over the course of many more years of learning—and I am still on that road—my faith has become the guiding light of my life.

The above account first appeared in *Journal of the American Scientific Affiliation*, Vol. 55, Number 3, September 2003, and is used with permission.

Francis S. Collins is a physician and geneticist and until 2008 was director of the National Human Genome Research Institute at the National Institutes of Health. His research team identified the genes for cystic fibrosis and neurofibromatosis, and collaborated with others to identify the gene for Huntington's disease. He has been a member of the American Scientific Affiliation for over twenty years. His 2006 book *The Language of God: A Scientist Presents Evidence for Belief* presents a lucid account of his personal testimony and the compatibility of God and science. In 2007 he was awarded the Presidential Medal of Freedom by President George W. Bush. He lives with his wife in Bethesda, Maryland, and in his spare time enjoys riding a motorcycle and playing his guitar.

14

The Conversion of a Skeptic

CHARLES W. COLSON

One hot summer night in August of 1973, I visited an old friend at his home outside of Boston. It was during the darkest days of Watergate. My whole world was being turned upside down.

My friend was a keen businessman who had worked his way to the top. President of one of the largest corporations in America in his early forties, he was a hard-charging man driven to succeed. I understood—I was just like him.

But when I had paid him a quick visit during a business trip several months earlier, I had been astonished to find him peaceful, calm, relaxed: dramatically different.

When I asked him about it, he answered with an extraordinary explanation: "I have accepted Jesus Christ." I had never heard anything like those words before, but I could not deny that he had changed.

So, this August night, though I couldn't admit it to anyone, I was seeking something—and I knew my friend might have an answer. Something was wrong in my own life. Something much more than Watergate; I was empty inside, groping for whatever meaning there was to life, if indeed there was any.

That night he told me about his encounter with Jesus Christ, how his life had been transformed. Then he picked up a book off a coffee table, opened it to a chapter titled "Pride" and began to read.

It was one of the extraordinary moments of my life. The words from that book—*Mere Christianity*, written by the great English scholar C. S. Lewis—ripped through the protective armor in which I had unknowingly encased myself for forty-one years. Lewis wrote about man's great sin—his pride—as a spiritual cancer.

The events of my own life flashed before me. I thought I had been driven by a desire to provide for my family, build a good law firm, serve my country. But in reality what I was doing all those years was feeding my pride, proving how good I was. Lewis convicted me that all my efforts had been in vain, that in my drive for the top I had missed the real pinnacle—to know God in a personal way.

As I left my friend's home that night, I accepted his gift of the copy of *Mere Christianity*. I was deeply moved by his testimony and by the chapter he had read—though I refused to show it. But as I got into my car, the White House tough guy—the hatchet man, or so the press called me—crumbled in a flood of tears, unable to drive, calling out to God with the first honest prayer of my life. That was the night Jesus Christ came into my life.

Over the next week I studied *Mere Christianity*. I underlined, made notes, even kept a yellow pad at my side with two columns—one headed "there is a God," the other headed "there is not a God." On another sheet of paper I had two more columns—"Jesus Christ is God"— "Jesus Christ is not God."

I read the book as if I was studying for the most important case I had ever argued. Lewis's logic was so utterly compelling that I was left with no recourse but to accept the reality of the God who is and who has revealed himself through Jesus Christ. *Mere Christianity* simply sets forth a powerful, rational case for the Christian faith in a wonderfully readable way.

Since then I have given out hundreds of copies of *Mere Christianity* and have met thousands whose lives have been transformed by it. It is the book God has used most powerfully in my life, apart from his own Word.

But I must warn you, it is not a book you can pick up and put down easily, nor is it a book you can read and return to being the same person you were before. For it masterfully presents the case for Christ. After reading it, the uncommitted person can only make a choice for or against him. In a choice for him, the reader will discover, as did Lewis himself in his own conversion, that "the hardness of God is kinder than the softness of man, and His compulsion is our liberation."

The above account is taken from the Introduction of an anniversary edition of *Mere Christianity* published by Barbour and Company, Inc., Westwood, New Jersey, and printed with the permission of Prison Fellowship 2007.

Charles W. Colson served as special counsel to President Nixon from 1969 to 1973. In 1974 he pleaded guilty to Watergate-related charges and served seven months in prison. In 1976, Colson founded Prison Fellowship Ministries in collaboration with many churches and denominations. For over thirty years he has worked to reform the criminal justice system. The royalties of his twenty-three books are donated to the work of Prison Fellowship Ministries. A graduate of Brown University and George Washington University Law School, he received the Templeton Prize for Progress in Religion in 1993.

15

An *Apologia* on the Way

James T. Como

I first discovered C. S. Lewis by way of an appreciative article by Jeffrey Hart (blessings upon him) in *National Review*. A junior in college and besieged (it seemed to me) for my belief, I thought when reading it, *Can this be? A professing, rational, polemically successful,* academic *Christian who, nonetheless, was the commanding figure in his field?* I would see for myself. Now in my sixties, I look back on more than forty years of continually reading C. S. Lewis with delight and gratitude, and I pray for the repose of his soul.

Lewis's literary criticism came first—the neglected *An Experiment in Criticism*—and I was undone. Its clarity, cogency, explanatory power, and, especially, its generosity of spirit prefigured what would recur again and again: Lewis is always fresh. I went on immediately to *The Great Divorce*, having no idea of its subject; it remains among my favorites. Within weeks my wife-to-be was giving me Lewis books, which, as hard now as it is to believe, were not easy to find in the mid-1960s. Alexandra had discovered the Morehouse-Barlow bookstore, now long-gone, on Forty-first Street just east of Fifth Avenue in Manhattan.

Reading Lewis, along with reading, thinking and talking *about* Lewis—these were like breathing pure oxygen, or rather like emerging from some depth into fresh air. Lewis was *my* discovery. Sometimes one discovers someone and really thinks that he has *discovered* that someone. So I was astonished to learn that there were many others like me and always had been. Thus did fourteen discoverers begin the New York C. S. Lewis Society in 1969, the oldest of such groups, still the largest, and still going strong. These good people, who over the years have come and gone but who mostly have come and stayed (and sometimes have been sneeringly, and falsely, derided as "cultists"), have been collective lab partners and would change my life, not least because among them are my dearest friends. As Lewis puts it, all along a secret Master of Ceremonies has indeed been at work.

I decided to write a master's thesis on *Perelandra* (and eventually a doctoral dissertation on Lewis); I traveled to what was then the Lewis Collection at Wheaton College (an aisle between two library bookshelves which, with its grated door at one end and wall at the other, resembled a monk's cell); I met Clyde S. Kilby, to whom we all owe so much; I traveled to Oxford (Lewis's cozy, quirky, fitting world, already quite faded forty years ago but even now, distantly, retaining great imaginative appeal); I met and became a lifelong friend of Walter Hooper, to whom we also owe so much; I taught Lewis to many students who have become lifelong readers; I wrote and lectured and opined on radio and television; I became someone regarded as knowing a great deal about Lewis; and now I am invited to write this essay. Who knew?

The progression seems to me at once both surprising and inevitable, in fact, providential. Now, of the many things I may assert of this experience, this one is enduringly true: it has been very great fun—always satisfying, frequently exhilarating, and often downright joyful. And I am certainly more capacious than I would have been without Lewis; like a great *magister* he enacted what the Greeks called *psychagogia*, "leading me forth" and enlarging my soul.

But here I must acknowledge a caveat. Lewis is far from my only master, although he is the most influential one. Could this be because he was my first? As a lifelong Catholic, I might have encountered Chesterton before Lewis instead of by way of him. Had that been the case, would the great GKC, now a strong second, have been what CSL became? And I do know that Lewis's influence is itself limited. I already craved argument before reading Lewis (though he certainly feeds that craving better than anyone else). Nor did he influence my love of Spanish or of rhetoric; in fact, I've been having a forty-year argument with CSL precisely about that oldest of liberal arts. He failed in his attempt to teach me to value William Morris, E. R. Eddison, and Sir Walter Scott, just as he was not among those who taught me to cherish, say, Thornton Wilder (who has enriched me in ways quite other than has Lewis), Walker Percy, Sigrid Undset, Robertson Davies, Bishop Sheen, Chaucer (whom Lewis vastly undervalues, I think), Dr. Johnson, fairy tales, beast fables, the Middle Ages, allegory . . .

And yet, as Lewis was teaching me very much about many things (especially those touchstones of his thought, so memorably phrased), I have watched his *habits* of mind and imagination. Lewis the journalist, essayist, and critic; the philosopher and historian; the diarist, letter-writer, and teacher; the public figure of public houses, walking tours, and devoted friendships; the lover of nature and of conversation with all sorts of folk—these Lewises have taught me *as a matter of habit* to make distinctions, to see through prejudices, to value things-as-they-are, to track down and to test the unexamined assumptions that underlie received opinion, neither taking the world for granted nor entirely trusting it, and . . . but better I allow Paul Holmer to say it, as he does so well in *C. S. Lewis: The Shape of His Faith and Thought* (my favorite interpretive book on CSL): "his own paragraphs are a sort of splendid conversation. . . . His books create, almost as Kierkegaard did, the living variety of paradigms. . . . Wisdom has to be read off the whole shape of his thought and is not one trick within it."

Toward the end of *The Allegory of Love*, Lewis said of one of his own favorites, Edmund Spenser, that "his work is one, like a growing thing, a tree . . . with branches reaching to heaven and roots to hell. . . . And between these two extremes comes all the multiplicity of human life. . . . To read him is to grow in mental health." In that light I believe I can claim for Lewis what I cannot say of any of the writers I mentioned above: there really is a Lewis for everyone. The Christian thinker, polemicist, and devotional writer (in all his various modes, especially the fictional one)—that is, Lewis the apologist, whose vast influence and popularity certainly have mitigated the influence of those other Lewises—seems to teach his readers what each of us needs most to learn. The particular lesson I needed most to learn was of Hope—and only the late John Paul II even approaches Lewis's achievement in that respect—nor, I believe, could one or many together have taught me to Hope as Lewis has, even had Lewis been my one-hundredth master.

Finally, throughout his work we see Lewis satisfying Alexander Pope's criterion for great poetry: "Something, whose truth convinced at sight we find, / That gives us back the image of our mind." That . . . *regression* . . . has come by way of *Sehnsucht*—Lewis's conception of, emphasis upon, and evocation of our longing for heaven. Because of this Joy (as Lewis calls it), I know that I belong Home, from time to time have recognized its call, and above all else desire to be there.

James T. Como holds advanced degrees in medieval English literature (Fordham University) and in language, literature, and rhetoric (Columbia University) and is a professor of rhetoric and public communication at York College in the City University of New York, where he has taught for forty years. A founding member of the New York C. S. Lewis Society (1969) and former editor of its bulletin, *CSL*, he has published *Remembering C. S. Lewis: Recollections of Those Who Knew Him* (Ignatius) and *Branches to Heaven: The Geniuses of C. S. Lewis* (Spence), as well as articles on Lewis in such journals as *National Review*, *SEVEN: An Anglo-American Literary Review*, *The Wilson Quarterly*, and *The New Criterion*. Dr. Como lectures widely on Lewis and other Christian authors. A native New Yorker, he and his Peruvian wife have two grown children and live in Westchester County, New York.

16

How Much I Didn't Know

Mary Coverdale

My family and I were the doorkeepers of our church for all of my growing-up years. Every time the doors opened, we were there, yet we didn't believe in an all-powerful, loving, redeeming God. Nobody talked about it, but we believed ourselves to be really good people. Even our minister declared one day, "I don't believe in the virgin birth." My dad said that our minister was the smartest man in the world, so as an eight-year-old I said to myself, *Well, I guess I don't believe in it either.*

Fast forward to age twenty-nine. I had three children and a wonderful husband whom I adored. The children had come in lightning-fast order, and one day it dawned on me that this "good" person needed help to be the calm, peaceful, and loving mother I wanted to be. Somehow I knew this help would have to come from the God I didn't believe in, but I hadn't the least idea how to find him.

It was amazing how much I didn't know, considering the hours I'd spent in church. I hadn't the slightest idea that I was a sinner separated from God and that I needed Jesus to close the gap. A sister-in-law had spoken the gospel to my deaf ears when I was newly married, but I hadn't heard a word she said. A few years later I received a small book in the mail, probably from her, but I know now that this gift was truly from God.

I read *Mere Christianity* and began to consider C. S. Lewis's explanation of right and wrong as a clue to the meaning of the universe. As Lewis's argument sank into me and took hold, I began to realize that the world had to have an author, and that this author had given me a law to obey, and I was not obeying it. I wanted God to somehow help me to be a good mother, but I quickly learned that his help would come with conditions, even with demands on how I behaved. It suddenly dawned on me that I could not simply reform myself. As Lewis puts it, I had to accept God's offer. He offered not only forgiveness but a new reality—actually becoming a child of God. He would put his Spirit in me, which would allow and help me to obey him. So, I gave in. I gave in to God's way.

And once I did, Joy became the substance of my life. I thought that I had been happy before, but suddenly Joy—something better than mere happiness—seemed to come bubbling out of me. I found myself singing all the time. I made up songs with my children about how God loves us. Another joy followed: my beloved husband also put his trust in the Lord. Soon after that, I laid in a stock of copies of *Mere Christianity* to share with others, knowing how much God had used that book in my life. I also wrote to the minister who did not believe in the virgin birth to let him know that I had found the source of real Joy. I never heard back from him.

Later, I discovered other Lewis books and read all of them that I could find. *The Great Divorce* became a favorite. Lewis there states that heaven is reality itself. All that is heavenly will remain because it is unshakable. Everything else will fall away. Lewis described the "thickening" process of learning, to want God for himself, not just as a means to an end. In this book I saw the awfulness of enslaving sin, as when the traveler sees the man with the red lizard on his shoulder and must kill it no matter what. And once he does, the monster on his shoulder becomes his servant. I saw from what I read that I would have to do the same with my own sins. If I wanted to be "sown a natural body [but] raised a spiritual body" (1 Cor. 15:44 KJV), then, as Lewis so vividly showed me, I would have to cast aside my earthly sins for the sake of heaven. I learned about how and why to try from Lewis, and I continue today to try to live my life in light of heaven.

My love for Lewis's writings caused all four of my children to become Lewis enthusiasts as well. We started by reading the Narnia tales aloud as we drove across the country in our 1964 station wagon. To my everlasting joy, the Lord has called each of our children and our ten grandchildren to the great adventure of knowing him and going, in the words of Lewis, "further up and further in." I can hardly count all of the ways that Lewis has so faithfully and creatively mentored me on my spiritual journey toward heaven.

Mary Coverdale grew up in Rochester, New York. After earning a degree in marketing from Syracuse University, she moved to California, where she met and married her husband, a successful rocket engineer. After several mission trips to Mexico, they sought a way to serve God full-time. In 1976 they started Calvary Missionary Press, a growing printing ministry that edits, maintains address lists, and prints newsletters for over 650 missionaries around the world. Mary's husband, J. Scott Coverdale, is a descendant of the Bible translator Miles Coverdale (1488–1569).

17

His Books Stirred an Unused Part of My Brain

Joy Davidman

By 1946 I had two babies; I had no time for Party (Communist) activity, and was glad of it; I hardly mentioned the Party except with impatience. And yet out of habit, I went on believing that Marxism was true. Habit, and something more. For I had no knowledge of divine help, and all the world had lost faith in gradual progress; if now, in the day of the atomic bomb, I were to lose my trust in violent means of creating heaven on earth, what earthly hope was there?

A year or so before this, my interest in fantasy had led me to C. S. Lewis—*The Screwtape Letters* and *The Great Divorce*. These books stirred an unused part of my brain to momentary sluggish life. Of course, I thought, atheism was *true*; but I hadn't given quite enough attention to developing the proof of it. Someday, when the children were older, I'd work it out. Then I forgot the whole matter. That was all, on the surface. And yet, that was a beginning.

Francis Thompson symbolized God as the "Hound of Heaven," pursuing on relentless feet. With me, God was more like a cat. He had been stalking me for a very long time, waiting for his moment; he crept, nearing so silently that I never knew he was there. Then, all at once, he sprang.

My husband had been overworking. One day he telephoned me from his New York office—I was at home in Westchester with the children—to tell me that he was having a nervous breakdown. He felt his mind going; he couldn't stay where he was, and he couldn't bring himself to come home. . . . Then he rang off.

There followed a day of frantic and vain telephoning. By nightfall there was nothing left to do but wait and see if he turned up, alive or dead. I put the babies to sleep and waited. For the first time in my life I felt helpless; for the first time my pride was forced to admit that I was not, after all, "the master of my fate . . . the captain of my soul." All my defenses—the walls of arrogance and cocksureness and self-love behind which I had hid from God—went down momentarily. And God came in.

How can one describe the direct perception of God? It is infinite, unique; there are no words, there are no comparisons. Can one scoop up the sea in a teacup? Those who have known God will understand me; the others, I find, can neither listen nor understand. There was a Person with me in the room, directly present to my consciousness—a Person so real that all my previous life was by comparison mere shadow play. And I myself was more alive than I had ever been; it was like waking from sleep. So intense a life cannot be endured for long by flesh and blood; we must ordinarily take our life watered down, diluted as it were, by time and space and matter. My perception of God lasted perhaps half a minute.

At that time, however, many things happened. I forgave some of my enemies. I understood that God had always been there, and that, since childhood, I had been pouring half my energy into the task of keeping him out. I saw myself as I really was, with dismay and repentance; and, seeing, I changed. I have been turning into a different person since that half minute, everyone tells me.

When it was over, I found myself on my knees, praying. I think I must have been the world's most astonished atheist. My surprise was so great that for a moment it distracted me from my fear; only for a moment, however. My awareness of God was no comforting illusion, conjured up to reassure me about my husband's safety. I was just as worried afterward as before. Now, it was terror and ecstasy, repentance and rebirth.

When my husband came home, he accepted my experience without question; he was himself on the way to something of the kind. Together, in spite of illness and anxiety, we set about remaking our minds. For obviously, they needed it. If my knowledge of God was true, the thinking of my whole life had been false.

I could not doubt the truth of my experience. It was so much the *realest* thing that had ever happened to me! And, in a gentler, less overwhelming form, it went right on happening. So my previous reasoning was at fault, and I must somehow find the error. I snatched at books I had despised before; reread *The Hound of Heaven*, which I had ridiculed as a piece of phony rhetoric—and, understanding it suddenly, burst into tears. (Also a new thing; I had seldom previously cried except with rage.) I went back to C. S. Lewis and learned from him, slowly, how I had gone wrong. Without his works, I wonder if I, and many others, might not still be infants "crying in the night."

Taken from *These Found the Way: Thirteen Converts to Protestant Christianity*, David Wesley Soper, editor, Philadelphia: Westminster Press, 1951, 22–24. Used with permission from Presbyterian Publications.

Joy Davidman (1915–1960) was a poet and novelist who converted to Christianity in part through reading C. S. Lewis. She received a B.A. at Hunter College (1934) and an M.A. (in English) at Columbia University (1935). Her first book of verse, *Letter to a Comrade*, won the Yale Series of Younger Poets Award for 1938. She also authored two novels: *Anya* and *Weeping Bay*. *Smoke on the Mountain, an Interpretation of the Ten Commandments*, was first published in 1955 with a foreword by C. S. Lewis. For a more complete account of Joy Davidman's life and marriage to C. S. Lewis see *And God Came In* by Lyle W. Dorsett and *Lenten Lands: My Childhood with Joy Davidman and C. S. Lewis* by Douglas H. Gresham.

18

The Writing of C. S. Lewis Has Changed My Life

Lyle W. Dorsett

Except for the Bible, no collection of writings has shaped my worldview and soul as much as the works of C. S. Lewis. Although I had long been familiar with Lewis's name and a few titles he had produced, it was not until about 1975 that I read anything he had written.

Lewis's profound impact on my life of faith in Jesus Christ goes back to my days as professor of history at the University of Denver. In 1974 or 1975, one of my students challenged me after class one day: "Sir, did I understand you to say that intelligent people are not Christians?" I replied, "No, I said that intelligent, *thoughtful* people are not Christians. They are agnostics." My student inquired if I had read any books by G. K. Chesterton or C. S. Lewis. I admitted that I had not. Within a few days he had purchased a copy of Chesterton's *Orthodoxy* for me.

Soon after, this young man talked me into reading some of C. S. Lewis's books. If I recall correctly, they were *Mere Christianity* and *The Screwtape Letters*. Soon thereafter he urged me to read *Surprised by Joy*. Then, in the autumn of 1975, I was on the University of Colorado campus and learned that Professor Clyde Kilby from Wheaton

College in Illinois was going to speak one evening on C. S. Lewis. I went and heard Professor Kilby speak, and he autographed for me one of the books he had written on Lewis. I do not remember what Kilby said, but I do know that his stories about his personal relationship with Lewis and his brother Warren intrigued me.

To make a long story short, Kilby's lecture and writings, several books by Lewis, and the witness and prayers of my wife and that University of Denver student, all conspired with some other factors to bring me to repentance and faith in the Lord Jesus Christ in the summer of 1976. In the wake of my conversion, I read more Lewis. Indeed, he became my teacher through his books, articles, and letters.

Sometime in 1980 I decided to write a biography of Lewis's wife, Helen Joy Davidman. My research took me to the Wade Collection at Wheaton College. I made contact with both of Joy's sons, her brother, and a first cousin who lived in Florida, which gave me access to a rich collection of Joy's letters. This biography of Joy caused Wheaton College to offer me Clyde S. Kilby's position at the Wade Collection when he retired in the early 1980s.

Serving as the curator of the Wade Collection and eventually as the director of the Wade Center opened opportunities for what I am tempted to call complete immersion in the writings and world of C. S. Lewis. Studying Lewis's life and writings (published and unpublished) opened my mind and enriched my soul. My career was shaped by my encounter with Lewis; certainly my love for the historic Anglican Church with its liturgy and sacraments has been another effect of Lewis's impact on me.

In summary, Professor Lewis played a major role (choreographed by the Holy Spirit, to be sure) in my conversion and spiritual formation as a Christian. Thanks to Lewis I have been introduced to dozens of authors who have influenced my thinking, and my wife and I have met people who have become friends and enriched our lives beyond measure.

Lyle W. Dorsett is the Billy Graham Professor of Evangelism at the Beeson Divinity School, Samford University, Birmingham, Alabama. He is the author of *And God Came In* (Macmillan, 1983), *C. S. Lewis: Letters to Children* with coeditor Marjorie Lamp Mead (Scribner, 1996), *Seeking the Secret Place: The Spiritual Formation of C. S. Lewis* (Brazos, 2004), *A Passion for Souls: The Life of D. L. Moody* (Moody Publishing, 2005), and numerous other works. He lives in Birmingham with his wife, Mary.

19

When the Science Is Fiction but the Faith Is Real

DAVID C. DOWNING

When I was about fifteen, I complained to my dad about people in our local church who were uptight, legalistic, and basically just uncool. My dad replied, "Well, David, I see you've mastered the easy part. You've noticed that too often, other Christians make disappointing ambassadors for the kingdom. Now I want you to work on the hard part—to yourself become an effective ambassador for the kingdom." I've spent most of my adult life trying to live out my father's advice, and I have found C. S. Lewis to be an admirable role model and mentor in this journey.

I grew up in a conservative church in Colorado Springs, the son of Jim Downing, an executive for the Navigators, and Morena Downing, a teaching leader in Bible Study Fellowship. The people in our church were mostly good-hearted folks, but they seemed to me too quick to settle for simple answers to life's most perplexing questions. As a boy, I never set out to be a naysayer or a rebel. But I just couldn't help asking questions, and I couldn't help feeling disappointed by the answers I got.

In fourth grade, for instance, I told my teacher one Sunday that there must have been a least one sincere seeker among the ancient Navajos or Mayans who would have responded to the gospel if given the chance. Would every single one of them spend an eternity in hell, I asked, just because Christian missionaries hadn't learned yet how to cross the Atlantic? (It would have been a different question whether the coming of Europeans to the New World turned out to be good news for the native peoples.) My Sunday school teacher replied that God knew in advance who would respond to the gospel, so he made sure to populate North and South America entirely with people who would have rejected Christian evangelism if given the opportunity. That was an ingenious answer but not a very emotionally satisfying one. Again, my dad was more helpful. In answer to the same question, he told me to worry less about the *mechanism* of salvation and to focus more on the *Author* of salvation. He said that a just and all-loving God does not make unfair or arbitrary judgments. He added that I didn't need to understand all the details of the divine plan as long as I could put my trust in the Divine Character.

By the time I reached high school, my faith was in doubt, and I was wrestling with all the usual questions: How could a good God create a world in which there is so much suffering and injustice? How could people who had never heard the gospel be consigned to eternal damnation? Why should all of humanity be blighted by the disobedience of two humans thousands of years ago? Why did our infallible Bible seem to have scientific errors or discrepancies between different accounts of the same event? Friends and family members gave me books and tracts to read on these topics, but I seldom found them helpful. They tended to answer easy questions I'd never thought of but passed over the hard questions I thought about all the time. For example, I never needed a rebuttal to the theory that Jesus just swooned on the cross and was later revived by his friends. What I wanted to know was, why couldn't a loving God just forgive our sins outright, without the whole bloody drama of the Passion?

It sounds odd to me now, but I grew up in a Christian home in the '50s and '60s without ever hearing about the Narnia Chronicles or their author. My older brother had a copy of *The Screwtape Letters* on his bookshelf, but it had a picture of a smarmy, smirking devil on its cover. I assumed this book must be full of dark and cynical observations. And I figured I had enough of those in my head already without having to seek out more. When I went off to college, I took an introductory literature course that included *Perelandra* on the syllabus, along with well-known works by William Shakespeare, Franz Kafka, and Leo Tolstoy. The classic works lived up to their reputations (at least for this budding English major). But it was the stranger in the crowd, *Perelandra*, that turned my world upside down (or, more accurately, turned it back right-side up). I knew the story had to do with interplanetary travel, so I was expecting a bit of "literary" science fiction along the lines of H. G. Wells or Isaac Asimov. What I wasn't expecting was a novel that would challenge me to reimagine my faith, that would tackle head-on some of the very questions that I had been grappling with since childhood.

Perelandra is the second book of the Space Trilogy (more accurately called the Ransom Trilogy). In the first book, *Out of the Silent Planet* (which I read after *Perelandra*), Lewis tells the story of Elwin Ransom, a Cambridge professor who is abducted and carried off to Mars. Despite his terrifying expectations, Ransom discovers that the inhabitants of Mars, who call their world Malacandra, are not at all like the nightmarish visions of his imagination. There are three rational species on the planet, very different from one another but all friendly and living in harmony. As a Christian, Ransom wonders if he should instruct these creatures in his faith, but rather it is they who show him what is actually going on in our corner of the cosmos. They explain that the solar system was created by the all-good Maleldil, but his viceroy on the third planet has turned into a rebel, taking his armies with him. The third world, our Earth, is now cut off from the others and thus is called "the Silent Planet." It remains a battleground, though there are rumors in Deep Heaven of wondrous things performed by Maleldil to reclaim his lost world.

This is certainly the stuff of science fiction. It is also orthodox Christian theology. By traveling to another world, Ransom discovers that what he thought of as his religion is simply reality. When reviews of *Out of the Silent Planet* were published, very few noticed the Christian worldview underlying the fiction. Lewis quipped that any amount of theology could be smuggled into readers' minds without their knowing it under the guise of romance. And in *Perelandra* he carried the process even further.

Unsuspecting reader that I was, when I picked up *Perelandra*, I had hopes of a good adventure story, never expecting light fiction to have much to say about my faith. Lewis begins this second book of the trilogy with himself as a character, trekking out to a remote cottage to meet his friend Ransom. "Lewis" had been told all about Ransom's adventures on Mars and suspected that his otherworldly friend was currently entertaining strange visitors here on Earth. Like Ransom on his way to Mars, "Lewis" is terrified about the prospect of meeting some creature not of this world. Despite his precautions, "Lewis" does encounter a majestic, awe-inspiring column of light that speaks to him, a being that seems more like a "thinking mineral" than a creature of flesh and blood. When Ransom returns from a brief absence, he assures "Lewis" that this magnificent being is benign, a faithful servant of Maleldil. Referring to the rebel eldils on Earth, Ransom quotes the verse from Ephesians about our having to wrestle with "spiritual wickedness in high places" (6:12 KJV). He goes on to explain that the New Testament Greek refers not to corrupt earthly leaders but to transphysical beings on a cosmic plane of existence.

At some point, hopefully it will flash into the mind of every reader: eldils are angels. Lewis has reimagined for us what it might feel like to actually encounter an angel. If Lewis had depicted a heavenly messenger clad in radiant garments, its identity would be so recognizable as to be dismissible. The word *angel* has been so overused that it may suggest nothing more than a Halloween costume or a cartoon character sitting on someone's shoulder. Lewis intended for his fiction to reenergize his readers' spiritual imaginations, to make *God* and *angel* and *soul* (and *heaven* and *hell*) terms of genuine wonder and terror, to make the Christian life a moment-by-moment cosmic adventure, not a once-a-week religious obligation.

In talking about the Narnia Chronicles, Lewis outlined the strategy that he also used in his science fiction trilogy. He said that he wanted to recast essential Christian doctrines into "an imaginary world, stripping them of their stained-glass and Sunday school associations," to "steal past those watchful dragons" of enforced reverence or tedious religious lessons. By enlisting the unfettered powers of imagination, Lewis hoped to recapture the original beauty and poignancy of the Good News. In this strategy, Lewis has been brilliantly successful in the hearts and minds of millions of readers, including me.

In *Perelandra* Lewis tells the story of Ransom's mission to Venus (Perelandra) and his battle to preserve that world in its unfallen, Edenic state. Apart from revivifying the reader's sense of the cosmic drama in which we all play a part, the novel also contains a profound meditation on the nature of good and evil. It suggests that we all carry Adam and

Eve around inside us, that we reach for the wrong fruit every day, and that we too often try to assert a godlike control over our own lives. Ransom's mission to preserve paradise is a success, and the story ends with his mystic vision of the great dance of creation, a cosmos full of dynamism and order that only seems "planless to the darkened mind, because there are more plans than it looked for."

Although I began reading *Perelandra* as a class assignment, I remember continuing far beyond the assigned pages, finishing the story late one night just as the college library was closing. As I walked back to my dorm room, my mind started playing tricks on me, and I began imagining that I might see eldils. I gave every peculiar slant of light a second look, thinking, *Why, that's only the moonlight filtering through the trees—and yet for a moment . . .*

After *Perelandra* I grabbed every book I could find with the name C. S. Lewis on the cover. I gobbled up the other two books of the Ransom trilogy and then started on the Narnia Chronicles. I read all seven chronicles in two weeks and then reread all seven in the next two weeks. Next came *Mere Christianity*, *The Problem of Pain*, and *Miracles*, in which I discovered the powerful intellect that accompanied Lewis's robust imagination. Lewis spent most of his teens and twenties as a militant atheist, so when he returned to Christianity, he knew only too well what the hard questions are and how they can best be addressed. And he was not afraid to say, "I don't know" about great questions that still contain a profound element of mystery.

After reading more than a dozen of Lewis's books in college, I eventually went back and hunted up the one with the smirking devil on it, and I found *The Screwtape Letters* delightful after all. Though I have now read all of Lewis's books, most of them many times, I will never forget my first experience of the Ransom trilogy. Lewis said that when he encountered George MacDonald's *Phantastes* as a teenager, that classic work of Christian fantasy provided a spiritual cleansing that baptized his imagination. Lewis's books have performed the same service for me. And sometimes, like Lewis himself, I am apt to look up at twilight, see the evening star, and whisper in wonder, "Perelandra!"

David C. Downing is the R. W. Schlosser Professor of English at Elizabethtown College, Elizabethtown, Pennsylvania. He has written numerous articles and books on C. S. Lewis. Among them are *Planets* *in Peril: A Critical Study of C. S. Lewis's Ransom Trilogy* (University of Massachusetts Press), *The Most Reluctant Convert: C. S. Lewis's Journey to Faith*, and *Into the Region of Awe: Mysticism in C. S. Lewis* (both from InterVarsity Press). He lives with his wife, Crystal, a Dorothy L. Sayers scholar, in Elizabethtown, Pennsylvania.

20

Seeing through the Eyes of My Heart

Denis Ducatel

The first book I read by C. S. Lewis was *Mere Christianity*. As a Frenchman, I was fascinated by Lewis's ability to make the Christian faith sound more rationally acceptable. I was a new Christian and was attracted to his abstract, philosophical works. Later, when I attempted to read Lewis's Narnia stories, I could not appreciate this type of fantasy literature. In fact, I strongly disliked it. Like many French people, I was cut off from any intuitive or imaginative way of knowing. This was also true for me with J. R. R. Tolkien's The Lord of the Rings; his fantasy novels left me cold.

Oddly, while translating Lewis's spiritual autobiography, *Surprised by Joy: The Shape of My Early Life*, into French, I experienced an inward reconciliation between my Cartesian French education and my underdeveloped imaginative and intuitive side. Whereas I had great skills in analyzing anything that came my way, I was able to keep faith at a distance. Personally (and I believe this is also true for people raised in the French culture in general), my rejection of symbols in literature had to do with the rejection of the feminine way of knowing. Most French students have to study René Descartes, and most of us overemphasize what is traditionally known as the more masculine way of approaching reality—the discursive, analytical, logical approach. Descartes, after all, invented analytic geometry, and such analytical approaches to thought hold great appeal for many French people.

In *Surprised by Joy* Lewis talked of a Joy that I did not understand. His idea of Joy was not found in traditional pleasures or emotional happiness but rather in a sense of longing for the unattainable, an unsatisfied desire. As I worked through the translation, my concept of longing for God, for beauty, and for heaven began to change. I began to appreciate my intuitive side; I was beginning to respond to God with my heart as well as my head, to imagine things that I couldn't appreciate before. Thanks to *Surprised by Joy* I felt a healing taking place in my way of approaching reality—through the imaginative world of Lewis! Now, I am seeing through the eyes of my heart. I now attend an Anglican church in Switzerland. I love the symbols and rich liturgy, something I didn't think possible before I learned from C. S. Lewis about this new way of looking at this life and longing for the next.

Denis Ducatel has translated the following works by C. S. Lewis into French: *Surprised by Joy*, *The Abolition of Man*, *The Great Divorce*, *The Four Loves*, *Letters to Malcolm*: *Chiefly on Prayer*, *The Problem of Pain*, and *Reflections on the Psalms*, all available through Editions Raphaël, Mont-Pèlerin. Fluent in German, English, and French, Mr. Ducatel also teaches English at the Ecole Hotelière in Montreux, the school that turns out charming managers for hotels around the world. In his spare time he enjoys visiting art galleries and gardens and cooking desserts.

21

Beyond the Stars

Colin Duriez

Somehow I missed out on the Chronicles of Narnia in my childhood, despite the fact that my younger brother and I were avid readers and worked our way through the children's section of the local library, sharing our discoveries. It was not until I was in the final years of grammar school in the English Midlands that I first came across the writings of C. S. Lewis in 1965. It was one of the great discoveries of my life. I was probably about eighteen years of age when we began reading *Mere Christianity* in a class intended to familiarize students with Christian teaching. I was immediately attracted by his compelling logic (having recently discovered philosophy with great excitement) and by the vivid analogies that he used to illustrate his arguments. I was already a believer, so I accepted Lewis's conclusions more readily than did most of my classmates. Then a friend, knowing my literary interests, informed me that the author of the slim paperback had written three very interesting science fiction stories. As with any author that I liked, I proceeded without any further ado to explore all the other books I could find by Lewis.

At that time his *Surprised by Joy* made a particular impact upon me as it contained his account of his "dialectic of desire"—his spiritual pilgrimage guided by his sense of inconsolable longing that he called Joy. The revelation of his experiences of Joy—linked as they were to the beauty of the natural world and to his wide reading of books—provided a sort of map for my own childhood and adolescent experiences. I understood them in a Lewisian way, not knowing then that he viewed his experiences through the writings of William Wordsworth, George MacDonald, and a great cloud of witnesses.

Surprised by Joy also supplied a kind of reading list, leading me to discover J. R. R. Tolkien's *The Hobbit* and The Lord of the Rings, and George MacDonald's books, *Phantastes* and *Lilith* in particular. Reading Lewis's letters, edited by his brother, Warren, extended my potential library, and I discovered Charles Williams with delight, filling my head with his doctrine of images and the two Ways of Affirmation and Negation.

Then, of course, there was Narnia. Since first encountering the snowy wood and following Lucy through the wardrobe as a young adult, I find that the land of Narnia has become a permanent part of my imagination. It is a vivid place, just like the countries I have lived in. Narnia's geography and its creator can be allegorized, even though Lewis did not create the Chronicles as allegory. Like Lewis himself, I prefer the story and its poetic vision, but the doctrines of Christianity such as the Narnian parallels with Christ, the universe as a created thing, and many others have enriched my understanding and perception of what are usually found in the contents of a volume of systematic theology. Along with such great and heady doctrines, Narnia also illuminates for me a Christian and classical moral worldview.

While in those early days I was exploring what Clyde S. Kilby happily called "the Christian world of C. S. Lewis," I heard Francis Schaeffer give a series of extraordinary and mind-opening lectures in London, before I left for two years of service in Turkey with an organization called Operation Mobilization, which would lead me to full-time study at the University of Istanbul. Schaeffer's lectures concerned patterns in Western thought leading to today's post-Christian world. When they were published soon afterward as *Escape from Reason*, I was enthralled. They gave me an inspiring and challenging new way of looking at the world. I saw a number of parallels with what I knew then of Lewis's thought.

Other thinkers I discovered around this time who helped me build upon what I was learning from Lewis included the art historian Hans

Rookmaaker, the philosopher Herman Dooyeweerd, and the polymath Michael Polanyi. All these played their part in shaping my basic understanding of the world—my worldview. As well as presenting pioneering views on symbolism and changes in human consciousness in history, Rookmaaker's study of art history gave a visual complement to Lewis's insights on literary history. Dooyeweerd represented the background and foundation of Rookmaaker's work, and his emphasis on the importance of ordinary knowledge and experience of the world, together with his view that the human being is structurally open and unspecialized, particularly attracted me. Polanyi made clearer the nature of human tacit knowledge, and also the fact that knowledge and reality are far richer than can be captured in the abstractions of scientific inquiry. I became particularly concerned with a characteristically Lewisian problem, the relationship between reason and imagination, an issue that preoccupies me to this day. As I write, I have just completed a contribution to a symposium on myth, imagination, and the Inklings.

Even among these thinkers—who I believe had a deep affinity—Lewis stood out in holding together the intellectual and the imaginative and in representing an ancient bookish culture. His thought and writings gave support to my love of books. Furthermore, his continual quest for the real thing—the distinctiveness of people, places, animals, moods, and seasons—resembled a similar pursuit of the real in the other thinkers I admired: Polanyi, Dooyeweerd, Schaeffer, and Rookmaaker. They all hunted aspects of the real, but Lewis seemed to have the bigger net for the capture. Lewis held the central place for me despite the fact that I knew Schaeffer and Rookmaaker personally. I had the benefit of being able to ask them questions and thus to draw upon the wealth of their knowledge and to benefit from their direct teaching. All this demonstrated to me the remarkable power of books. Though I never met Lewis (he died while I was still a schoolboy), his beautifully written books nurtured my mind, imagination, and spiritual life. He taught me, even more importantly, that writers who lived centuries or even millennia ago could nurture us today. Since I first discovered Lewis, the heart of my learning and scholarship has been associated with books (which is in no way to deny the scientific enterprise and the growth of knowledge through experiment and hypothesis). My life after university has been a life in books, for many years as a commissioning editor with InterVarsity Press in the United

Kingdom and later mainly as a writer. And, of course, as a Christian, I am a person of the Book.

People sometimes ask me if I tire of writing and speaking on Lewis and other Inklings, such as Tolkien. The truth is that I find them endlessly fascinating and feel that I have only paddled in a great ocean (to use Lewis's words about reading Tolkien). Not only is there in Lewis that sense of the depth of reality, but also his insights and continuing presence through his books make other thinkers and writers who seem to have an affinity constantly inspiring, including those who were important to me in the early days of my acquaintance with Lewis's writings and whom I associate with him. Since those early days, of course, I've encountered many other writers and thinkers who have nourished me on the way. But, thanks in large part to Lewis, the focus has always remained on a larger kingdom—the divine rule of Christ—which transcends all civilizations and all books. Thanks also to Lewis—and those other thinkers—this kingdom is not merely an abstraction but is also something gloriously real and tangible which demands my total commitment and opens up endless possibilities. It wasn't Lewis, but Schaeffer, who once said (and it goes to the heart of Lewis's vision): "The Christian is one whose imagination should fly beyond the stars."

Colin Duriez has published a number of books on C. S. Lewis and his fellow Inklings, including *The C. S. Lewis Encyclopedia*, *The Inklings Handbook* (with David Porter), *Tolkien and C. S. Lewis: The Gift of Friendship*, *A Field Guide to Narnia*, and *The C. S. Lewis Chronicles*. His other books include *AD 33: The Year That Changed the World*, *Field Guide to Harry Potter*, and *Francis Schaeffer: An Authentic Life*. He has also lectured on Lewis and the Inklings in a number of countries, including the United States and Canada. He lives in England's Lake District.

22

A Pastor for My Need

Martha Atkins Emmert

By 1958, well into my first missionary term in Africa, my faith floundered. Measuring my unproven abilities against the enormity of my job's demands, I feared that I had jumped into something over my head. With rising panic and without a pastor or confidant to whom I dared confess such disastrous fears, I searched for help among the libraries of my colleagues. In one of them, God pointed out *Mere Christianity*. As I read the successive chapters, life came back into perspective; the commitment I had made seemed possible to fulfill. From then on, C. S. Lewis served as my pastor and counselor, and I have been avid and relentless in my acquisition of any words he wrote or said.

In retrospect, I realize it had been a long time since I had had a pastor. In seminary I was active in fieldwork on Sundays, serving as a junior church leader and therefore seldom hearing a sermon. In Belgium, where my husband, Leon, and I were studying French in preparation for going to Congo, I found little spiritual comfort in the church we attended. In Africa I, the missionary, found myself floundering in my own sea of need.

Lewis brought back all the faith-building truths I needed in terms that comforted and delighted me. He never used the religious jargon that had bothered me so much as a converted pagan. I clung to his words as to a lifeboat. I was a lone shepherd floundering at my job when help appeared. C. S. Lewis reassured me that God was there for me. He taught me that it wasn't so much new truths that I needed but the frequent reminder of the same old truths and duties that one tires of and neglects—the duty of trust and obedience that I am so apt to carelessly forget and shirk.

As I read, life came back into perspective. The commitment I had made now seemed possible to fulfill. Tears blurred my vision as Lewis's sympathy and understanding brought comfort, healing, and hope. He encouraged me to "Keep on, doing what you can."

I remember when my daughter in her early teens found her mother an embarrassment, we who had been so close. How could I bear it? Lewis cut cleanly with his sharp words of truth. He wrote of the tyranny of some women whose need to be needed ruins the lives of others. A golden opportunity opened to me—dying to self. A desperate solution, yes, but it caused me to show my love to my daughter by letting go.

In the years that followed I have used Lewis's books to counsel and guide. When I discovered *The Business of Heaven*, a book of devotional readings from Lewis's writings, I found a daily useful treasure. Lewis brings me back and back again to the task at hand, no matter how menial the duty of the day. C. S. Lewis steadied and sustained me through our thirty-five-year career in Congo and comforts me still today.

Martha Atkins Emmert was born in Muscatine, Iowa, into a family of seven, and as she describes it, "lived a nomadic life due to the Depression and our poverty." A high school dropout, she had despaired of a brighter future until she met Christ at eighteen. God gave her a purpose for living and made education possible by giving her the attitude, "I can do all things through Christ." In 1997 she published her autobiography, *Common Clay*. Now in her eighties, Martha lives with her husband in Fort Wayne, Indiana. They have two children, two grandchildren, and a great granddaughter.

23

A Life Mended by Velveted Paws

Paul F. Ford

I am a 1947 Ford. The year 1959 was the pivotal year of my early life. My parents were experiencing great unhappiness in their marriage, and they learned to medicate the pain of life with ever-increasing quantities of alcohol. One of their drinking partners, a constant visitor to our home and a friend to the Ford children, was a priest; he molested me. My "hundred years of winter" began.

Unable to confide in anyone, I carried this burden into a minor seminary (four years of high school and two years of college) hundreds of miles away from home. While there, my Latin teacher, Father George Crain, S.J., introduced me to the writings of C. S. Lewis. At a conference he preached in chapel from the devil's perspective about how to tempt seminarians, especially against charity, for we were being particularly unkind to a fellow who had an unusual gait and manner. When I praised Father Crain for his insights, he told me rather bashfully that he "stole" them from an Anglican, C. S. Lewis, in a book called *The Screwtape Letters*. On my next trip to a bookstore I was unable to find that book, but I bought *The Great Divorce*, still my favorite Lewis book. It gave me hope. I went on to read and reread everything by Lewis that I could get my hands on, mostly the apologetic works, but I also loved the Ransom trilogy.

Father Crain's greatest gift was the time he spent with me. Sometimes in the evenings I would walk down to his Jesuit residence and buzz the doorbell three short times (his code), and downstairs he would come; we would spend an hour together at least once a week, if not more, for four years. Together we read G. K. Chesterton's books and essays, and Greek plays in translation. We looked at books of photography, and he taught me to meditate on the images from nature and from life that we saw in them. During the summer between minor seminary and major seminary, I found out that Lewis had written a set of children's books. I bought but hid them, afraid of what my peers might think.

The day came when a bad cold sent me to bed for a week. I removed the Chronicles of Narnia from their hiding place and thus crossed a frontier into a world where I was at home. At first they made a strong appeal to my more apologetic side: they gave explanations of all that I held most dear. But as the years and the rereadings went on, I found myself returning to Narnia at times of crisis and recommending them to everyone I cared about. I began to know in my bones why Lewis said, "Reason is the natural organ of truth; but imagination is the organ of meaning." Lewis's fairy tales helped me to experience truth and meaning together and to experience the desirable, as J. R. R. Tolkien also taught me.

In major seminary I met my mentor, Monsignor O'Reilly—a philosopher, a theologian, and a Cal Tech physicist. I visited with him nearly daily, wearing out his doorstep. It was he who introduced me to the book *The Weight of Glory and Other Addresses*.

When Monsignor suffered a stroke in the early 1970s, I readily accepted the task of assisting him during his weeks of recovery. During his convalescence I persuaded him to read the Chronicles. He found the stories wonderful, and I cherish my copies with the pages that he dog-eared.

In the winter of 1977–1978, when I was making the difficult transition from life as a Benedictine monk to life "in the world," the meaning beneath the apologetic of the Chronicles overtook me. During this time I fell ill for a week and took up these books for perhaps the fifteenth time. Little did I know that I was not only being nourished in the depletion I was then feeling, but I was also being prepared for a loss greater even than my temporary loss of vocational direction, for Monsignor died suddenly in the spring of 1978. On the day, weeks later, when we cleared out his rooms completely, I could not rest for the abandoned feeling I felt. As I lay down to what I thought would be another fruitless nap, I remembered Shasta's experience with Aslan at the ancient tombs in *The Horse and His Boy*. The only prayer I could manage was, "Aslan, lie at *my* back. The desert is ahead of me, the tombs behind. Help me rest." And for the first time in months, I rested.

The rest of my story we will have to talk about in heaven. Suffice it to say this: C. S. Lewis gave me hope. C. S. Lewis taught me how to pray, to tell God my sorrows, to unveil myself before God, to show God who I am and what I desire, to welcome God's loving gaze and touch. A life marred by drunken groping was mended by velveted paws.

Paul F. Ford is professor of systematic theology and liturgy at St. John's Seminary, Camarillo, California (1988–present). From 1961–1973 he studied for the priesthood for the then-diocese of Monterey-Fresno but was never ordained. He was a Benedictine monk at St. Andrew's Abbey, Valyermo, from 1973–1978. Ford was the first Roman Catholic in the doctoral program in theology at Fuller Theological Seminary (Pasadena, California). His dissertation was: "C. S. Lewis: Ecumenical Spiritual Director: A Study of His Experience and Theology of Prayer and Discernment in the Process of Becoming a Self." In 1974 he founded the Southern California C. S. Lewis Society. Ford's award-winning *Companion to Narnia* (HarperCollins) is now in its fifth edition. On the dedication page he wrote: "In memory of George Crain, S.J. (1920–2003), who introduced me to C. S. Lewis, and James D. O'Reilly (1916–1978), who was C. S. Lewis to me." There is a world in those two clauses. He is married to Janice Daurio, Ph.D.

24

It's about God, Not Us

George Gallup Jr.

I first read C. S. Lewis's classic *Mere Christianity* when I was a sophomore studying in the Department of Religion at Princeton University in 1950. Although already a believer and powerfully drawn to Jesus, I was aware that often the strongest faith is a challenged one, and so I explored the treasures of the world's great religions through my elective courses.

In reading *Mere Christianity* as part of a course dealing with Christian classics, I was thrilled to discover that there can be a rational foundation for believing in the full divinity of Jesus. The high point of my reading—an epiphany, if you will—came when I read the passage where Lewis points out that we must conclude that Jesus was either God (as he claimed), a madman, or a liar. When I read those words while sitting in my bedroom one night, I remember saying aloud, "My God, it really is all true!"

Lewis's words on "the shocking alternative" are an important reminder to people at all times, as are his insights on other aspects of Jesus's divinity. They certainly are words for the present time when the gospel is being watered down—at least in the Western world—and the true nature and purpose of Jesus are being denied.

As always, the vital question facing the world is what we believe about Jesus Christ. Lewis's words should remain in the forefront of our thinking. I would imagine that *Mere Christianity*—and this passage in particular—may have transformed and converted more people in the world than nearly all other Christian books.

When we accept "the shocking alternative," as Lewis put it, life takes on new dimensions, and we see God at work in the daily lives of people in thrilling ways.

While Lewis provided me with a rational or logical basis for faith, he was also quick to remind me that faith often comes before, not after, understanding. In fact, Lewis said we should test this proposition for ourselves, and, if we are not believers, to act as if we did believe, and discover the new world of God's truth.

Lewis constantly reminds me to concern myself with God's agenda, not mine; life is about God, not me. One of the most powerful statements ever made by Lewis, I believe, comes at the very end of *Mere Christianity*. These are words I have never forgotten—words that remind me that in order to save my life, I am to lose it, in God. This is how we discover the meaning of life.

> Give up yourself, and you will find your real self. Lose your life and you will save it. Submit to death, death of your ambitions and favourite wishes every day and death of your whole body in the end: submit with every fibre in your being, and you will find eternal life. Keep back nothing. Nothing that you have not given away will ever be really yours. Nothing in you that has not died will ever be raised from the dead. Look for yourself, and you will find in the long run only hatred, loneliness, despair, rage, ruin, and decay. But look for Christ and you will find Him, and with Him everything else thrown in.

George Gallup Jr. is founding chairman of The George H. Gallup International Institute, established in memory of his father, George H. Gallup. The mission of the institute is "to discover, test, and implement new ideas for society in the areas of education, health, the environment, and religion and values." George Gallup holds a degree in religion from Princeton University. In 1954 Mr. Gallup joined the Gallup Poll, which was started by his father in 1935. He retired in 2004. Although Mr. Gallup was actively involved with the Gallup Poll for most of his professional life, the focus of much of his work over the years has been on religion and spirituality. He is the author or coauthor of numerous books, including *The Gallup Guide—Reality Check for Churches in the 21st Century*, *The Next American Spirituality*, and *Surveying the Religious Landscape*.

25

Never More Deeply Happy

Janine Goffar

Oh, brother. Another English essay assignment. That will blow the whole Saturday night. Such was my response one stifling September afternoon while sitting restlessly in freshman English Composition at my small, church-run college near St. Helena, California, and listening to tall, lanky Dr. Johnson give the particulars of our assignment: write an essay contrasting a piece by the English philosopher C. E. M. Joad, an atheist for most of his life, and a piece by C. S. Lewis. I'd never heard of either author, but I mused about how the British must go in for initials.

I had little interest in English or essays at that time; my goal was to get my nursing degree as quickly as I could. I finished the assignment, a shoddy piece of work I'm sure. Yet something happened to me while skimming those two contrasting pieces. The name C. S. Lewis became important to me. I realized that I was reading Really Worthwhile Stuff. I tucked his name into the back of my mind and determined that one day, when I had more time, I would pick up that book again—*Mere Christianity*.

Finally, I landed my dream post: a job as nurse on a cruise ship. The shipboard experience was everything I had dreamed of—travel, meeting people, exotic ports of call, beaches, sailing, and, most of all, the ocean itself. Clouds. Weather. Churning waves. Ever-changing scenes of magnificent natural beauty just off the deck and outside my porthole. I was giddy with joy. Yet I knew I wanted to make good use of my time outside working hours, to accomplish something besides sunbathing and stargazing.

Finding no books by C. S. Lewis in the ship's library, I decided to look for a Christian bookstore at our first port of call, Hamilton, Bermuda. Happily, there was one right near the dock. I was disappointed that it didn't have *Mere Christianity*, but it had another book by C. S. Lewis, *Surprised by Joy*. Okay, I thought, this'll do. I love biographies, and I especially love autobiographies.

The first few chapters were rough sailing, since I was unacquainted with the literary figures Lewis was mentioning. I felt I was in over my head. I stuck with him, however, and soon began to realize that Lewis might be talking about a recurrent experience I'd had in my own life, starting about the age of three when, while lying on my back in our yard, I discovered the night sky for the first time. I had never shared these experiences with anyone; I had never thought I could find words for them. A new word entered my vocabulary—or, rather, an old word gained a new and wondrous meaning—Joy.

In the margin of my book, in the chapter "Renaissance," I wrote: "Could Lewis's Joy be the desire for God, which contains, at the same moment, the presence of God? Could this mean that the mere desire for God is 'more desirable than any other satisfaction'? Could it be that all natural beauty was created for one main purpose—to inspire Joy, that is to say, to inspire the desire for God?"

I walked the deck with a feeling in my heart closer to my feelings on the day I was baptized at age eleven than anything I had known since. It was what Lewis had finally given me words for: a stab, a paradoxical pang of both longing and fulfillment, of both deepest desire and utter satisfaction. A "memory of a memory," which now became a new experience of profound heartbreak and joy. "The desire of all nations" (Hag. 2:7) and "the chair in which only one can sit" (*The Pilgrim's Regress*).

I do not know how long I circled the ship on the promenade deck trying to assimilate this new understanding of my own life—this present experience which was becoming one with many past experiences. Finally, I sat down on a deck chair, pleasantly exhausted, and prayed; I was completely alone on that gloriously sun-washed deck, yet never less alone or more deeply happy in my whole life.

Many more ports followed, with more shore excursions to find Christian bookstores. I couldn't get enough Lewis books. I couldn't get enough of my new friend and the things he was teaching me.

It's not like I was a prodigal returning home. I had been blessed with a mother and father who wore their Seventh-day Adventist religion lightly yet wholeheartedly. Mom was a nurse; Dad was a pastor. They were practical people above all, and they raised my sister and me with reasonable guidelines and humble religious assertions. They were open at all times to our questions and challenges, chuckling with us at what we saw as potential inconsistencies in the Bible or our religion, and they searched for answers right along with us. There was little need to rebel: if God was as loving (and sometimes impish) as my father and mother were, I knew I was in good hands.

But something *was* missing. Christianity had been the wallpaper of my life since birth, yet like wallpaper long lived with but now nearly invisible, I would have had trouble describing it to someone else.

Thus far, I'd had little need to describe it to anyone. Adventist children mostly go to Adventist schools and attend Adventist churches and social functions through their college years. As in all such insular worlds, we hardly knew what "outsiders" thought about, let alone what questions they might have. Now here I was, in one of the most secular environments imaginable, surrounded not by skeptics so much as people for whom religion was passé, a relic for museums. Something people did a long time ago in a less enlightened age. If they knew I was a Christian at all, most of the ship's officers with whom I ate and spent my time probably just hoped I'd keep it to myself.

At that time I could have given anyone an in-depth Bible study on why I kept Saturday as Sabbath instead of Sunday, or why I didn't believe we Adventists went straight to heaven or hell when we died. But how did I know there was a heaven? Why was I a Christian and not an atheist or agnostic—or, for that matter, a Buddhist? Why would a good God allow so much suffering in the world? These were things to which I had given little real thought.

In that sense I had a borrowed religion. C. S. Lewis helped me make it my own. He helped me formulate answers to the deepest questions, first in my own mind, and then, when the opportunity arose, to offer these answers to others. Lewis gave me a greater realization of why Jesus would be the very first person I'd want to see when I got to heaven—not Mother, not Dad, nor even Lewis himself. Lewis helped me understand I would find them all in God—that God is our true

Beloved, and the reason we love any earthly human is because some godly qualities reside in them.

I am certain I became rather insufferable during that period, because I couldn't stop quoting C. S. Lewis. But enough people indulged my new passion that I remained undeterred, and a few seemed genuinely interested. Our hard-bitten atheist chief engineer, who used to jeer at me, began to sit with me at mealtimes and to ask serious questions. His wife came on board for a few weeks and began to read Lewis herself. We lost touch, so I do not know where this led. But God knows. A deck officer to whom I loaned Lewis's books eventually became a Christian, married a Christian woman back in Holland, and the two planned to go out as missionaries. A worship group that started among the Indonesian and Filipino crew members took hold, spread to all the ships of that line, and continues.

But best of all, my own life and religious experience were transformed by meeting C. S. Lewis, and through him getting to know my Lord in a new, more mature, yet deeply personal way. I can hardly wait to thank—well—both of them, in person.

As a result of **Janine Goffar**'s passion for remembering C. S. Lewis passages, she started to create an index for herself. After ten years of work, this led to the 675-page volume *The C. S. Lewis Index* (Crossway Books, 1995). Janine Goffar lives in Loma Linda, California, where she continues nursing and freelance writing.

26

Coming to Faith by Way of Mars

David Good

All of my life I have loved reading, especially science fiction and (to a lesser extent) fantasy. One of my favorite books when I was growing up was *The Princess and the Goblin* by George MacDonald. In fact, I still have the family copy on the bookshelf behind me. I didn't really connect it to the Christian instruction I was getting—I just loved the story. I remember fairly early reading C. S. Lewis's Space Trilogy, which also connected with my interest in science fiction.

I read several other C. S. Lewis books, such as *Pilgrim's Regress* and *Mere Christianity*, but it was when I read *The Great Divorce* and found George MacDonald popping up as a character, with Lewis pointing to him as one of *his* formative influences, that things connected for me. I remember thinking, *Wow, C. S. Lewis likes George MacDonald, just like me!* and that gave his books added weight in my thinking.

Backing up a little, when I was growing up I had the usual church-oriented Christian instruction and was a regular churchgoer, but I think that my intellectual understanding of the content of faith never quite connected to an impulse to act on that understanding. When I went away to college, I found it hard to get motivated to go off campus to find a church to attend, and I pretty much stopped going. I was still reading science fiction, but I branched out to reading everything I could find by Lewis. This eventually brought me to a point of decision during my sophomore year at college, when I asked myself, *If I believe that the facts about Jesus of Nazareth are true, doesn't that mean that I should commit to obeying him as my Lord?*

I would have been around nineteen at that point, and I was walking across the quad at Rensselaer Polytechnic Institute in Troy, New York. Since that time, I think I have always been moving forward, keeping that resolution (although not always moving forward very fast). Rereading Lewis (and G. K. Chesterton, MacDonald, and Charles Williams) every few years is one of the things that brings that resolution back to my mind and recharges my energy.

After studies at Rensselaer Polytechnic, **David Good** earned a Ph.D. in physics at the University of Illinois. He currently works on developing software for medical X-ray CT scanners for the Toshiba Medical Research Institute. He and his wife, Nancy, have two grown children and live in Naperville, Illinois. He enjoys taking walks in the evening, especially to his local public library.

27

Making Me a "Mere" Christian

LEONARD G. GOSS

Although I am Jewish by blood, I was raised in the American Southwest without religious training or inclination of any kind. Almost no books lay around the house; my upbringing also lacked much of an intellectual life. I became a Christian in high school not long after I began attending Young Life meetings. This was a rather popular club at my school, and it drew many students. At that time I did not know that Young Life was a Christian ministry actively seeking to introduce students to Jesus Christ. At first I didn't think very much of the Christian messages, but I had a lot of fun hanging around with my friends at these interesting and entertaining gatherings.

I became very active in this club, and at the beginning of my sophomore year I was asked to join Campaigners, the Bible study group for the more serious Young Lifers. In a gradual change of heart and mind, I grew into an acceptance of Christianity. From a tradition of religious illiteracy, I began to understand Christianity through Bible study and Christian fellowship. Initially, the New Testament proved a very foreign and curious thing to me. Yet, by the middle of the school year, I realized with much amazement that I was reading the Bible as an out-and-out believer in Jesus Christ. For me, the conversion process didn't occur in a memorable moment or with the praying of a single prayer, but rather through a commitment to reading the gospel story through the eyes of a faith that I was coming to believe—a demonstration of the power and importance of Scripture.

Still, I needed additional tutoring in the faith. I went off to college, and during an undergraduate literature class, we read an essay by Bertrand Russell on why he was not a Christian. For Russell, an extreme controversialist, all religion was superstition based primarily and mainly on fear. He used cold and devastating logic to question not only the existence of God but also the historicity of Jesus. This troubled and perplexed me in my young faith, and I told the professor so. She recommended that I look at an alternative view of faith in the writing of C. S. Lewis. Though I had never heard of Lewis before, I found a collection of his essays and took several in hand, including "The Grand Miracle," "Christian Apologetics," "Religion: Reality or Substitute?" "God in the Dock," and "On Ethics." The depth and breadth of this man's thinking stunned me. To my mind, Lewis demolished Russell's arguments by showing how to justify Christianity on intellectual grounds. One could be a Christian without one's mind getting in the way. In Lewis I discovered a serious Christian supernaturalist who was a formidable intellect, polymath scholar, and sensitive wordsmith. Had this man written other things? I found out he had, and soon "Jack" Lewis became my mentor of the spirit, the mind, and the imagination. I thought I was the first person ever to discover *Mere Christianity*, and I talked about it to everyone! I read all things Lewis. He brought me a sense of wonder and a desire to enter the fray and strike blows for the kingdom.

Lewis has had this sort of spiritual and intellectual impact on many thousands of readers all over the world. During my graduate years in a Chicago divinity school, I could hardly find a student who had not been influenced by the Oxford don. I have also found this to be true in the church at large. On the topic of defending the Christian faith by using reason, no one opened more eyes than Lewis. He prepared multitudes inside both the intellectual community and the church for the type of intellectual warfare found in the marketplace of ideas. And yet, as a reading of *Surprised by Joy* will show, he was actually common, direct, accessible, and approachable.

How has C. S. Lewis affected my life? He has meant to me what W. T. Kirkpatrick, the Great Knock, meant to Lewis himself. Reading Lewis has not altered my personality or released me from any mental demons. Lewis's books have not made me smarter or more holy. But his prose taught me to think things through logically and to understand that faith and reason can coexist, that the mind and the heart should unite, and that the origin of ideas matters much. Also, Lewis reminds me that as a Christian I am a servant and that I sometimes have a price to pay for that servanthood. Lewis has helped me sift through countless moral and religious questions, and he challenges me to think Christianly and to grow spiritually. His fiction in its many forms has challenged my imagination to a vividness and reality regarding the world of the unseen and the cosmic struggle going on between heaven and hell. Lewis's books challenge me to hold doggedly consistent values, which I try to do, and to be who I really am—an ordinary person and no prima donna. I think that was Lewis's greatest gift to me, teaching me I am but a "mere" Christian. But then, so was Jack.

Leonard G. Goss has worked in book publishing for over three decades and is responsible for contributing a dozen books to the field of Lewisania, including *Jack's Life* by Douglas Gresham, *Further Up and Further In* by Bruce Edwards, and *Lewis Agonistes* by Louis Markos. He lives with his wife Carolyn (who teaches seminars on C. S. Lewis) in Franklin, Tennessee. They have two adult sons and three granddaughters.

28

Hearing the Truth for the First Time

Merrie Gresham

At the age of forty, I had achieved all of my life's dreams. I had a devoted husband, four healthy school-aged children, no financial worries, and a prosperous dairy farm in Tasmania, where we owned both the house and the farm outright. Though I should have been happy, I was strangely disconcerted and felt empty inside; my life seemed to lack any meaning or purpose.

Every day I would pretend to be happy and in control; I was good at pretending, and outward appearances formed a very important part of my deception. I had to look appealing personally, and my home and my garden had to conform to the *Better Homes and Gardens* ideal. I sought human approval: I was nice to people so that they would think I was a nice person and would love me. I fooled most of them.

But the truth was that I was full of bitterness and self-pity inside. I felt as though people took advantage of me, using me as their personal maid. And so I kept myself always busy, always listening to music. I especially loved listening to books on tape; that way I didn't have to think about my inner emptiness and my frustrations.

During this time, I stood vehemently against anything having to do with Christianity. If anyone dared to talk to me about God, let alone Jesus, I instantly crossed that person off my social list and was left with a feeling of intense irritation. You see, I felt as though I had been ill-used as a child because of the religious rules and regulations enforced upon me. I felt that I had been abandoned by my mother, for she seemed to spend most of her life at Mass or other religious functions.

God had designs upon me, however, and he was able to penetrate the strong defenses I had erected against him. His approach was very subtle, and I did not detect him until it was too late for me to put up a fight—and this is how he did it.

Without even realizing it, I had married the stepson of the world's most famous Christian apologist, C. S. Lewis. The only evidence of that in our lives was that our bookshelves were crammed full of his writings. But I seldom ever read, and these books were full of "God stuff," a taboo subject for me.

Adding to this collection of religious writings, one day a set of tapes of one of Lewis's books, *Mere Christianity*, found its way into our house as a gift. Although I loved listening to books on tape, this set collected dust on top of Lewis's other writings until one day, out of sheer boredom, I ventured to play them. Even still, I had my finger on the STOP button throughout the whole first tape. I wasn't about to take any "come-to-Jesus" stuff from anybody, not even from my husband's stepfather.

In the days that followed, I listened to all ten of those tapes. As I did, I had a strong feeling that I was hearing the truth for the first time in my life. Rather than "Churchianity" or religion, I was hearing about Christianity, and it felt strangely exciting. I longed for it to be real, for if it was real, I had found in Jesus a person who could really love me and accept me for what I was; I could drop my pretense of being happy and in control.

As months passed, I listened to those tapes over and over again. I even bought myself a Walkman just for that purpose. I had the headphones plugged into my ears wherever I went. I thought and thought about the concept of God's purpose for our lives and about the possibility that he could notice me and love me.

I could not conceive that God could love me. I thought that if he really knew me as well as I knew myself, he couldn't possibly love me. I knew myself to be full of bitterness, resentment, anger, and intolerance, which would sometimes come out in fits of rage. Mostly, though, I hid my real self.

And so, with regret and some sadness, I dismissed the whole subject and heaved a sigh of relief, for I thought that I had nearly been sucked into believing illusion and falsehood once again. But despite my conclusion, God himself was about to intervene in a dramatic way.

One day I had a very vivid waking dream—almost like an out-of-body experience, for I was fully awake at the time. I experienced a series of short dreams which were like the acts of a play wherein God showed me how, through loving someone, I could experience their pain as if it were my own; I could experience the "me" inside of them.

Next, God showed me that he himself is at the center of the "me" in every human being. I realized that God feels everything that I feel, both physically and emotionally. Like me, he longs for my well-being and happiness. He even shares my longings to be loved and accepted, to be comfortable and healthy, and to be of worth. He also shares my longing to be rewarded for my self-sacrifice and my effort. Moreover, he himself knows how to fulfill these longings much better than I do.

I also realized through this waking dream that other people also have God at the center of their "me," whether they know it or not. If I hurt someone, God feels their pain; if I am nice to someone, I am being nice to him, because he feels their pleasure.

So I came to realize that God does love me and to understand how it happens. I came into a relationship with God's love through that door of understanding.

At the very moment that I grasped the extent and meaning of God's love, something wonderful happened to me, something hard to put into words. I had never before experienced such happiness and joy as I felt then. I was accepted and loved by the most important person in the whole world, and therefore I could drop the pretense that I had lived all my life.

I then went through a very real form of repentance as I realized all the people I had hurt in my life and all of the relationships I had damaged. I was deeply ashamed, and I resolved never to behave that way again.

I knew that God was real by the way he had changed my whole life around. And I also knew that he had been waiting for me to come to this point in my life for a very long time.

So I accepted God's love for me, and it was the most meaningful thing I have ever done in my life. Very soon I began to read the Bible, something I had violently shied away from in the past. I now delighted in reading about Jesus's salvation plan for me. The words of Matthew 25:40 were of particular interest to me. Having been brought up a Catholic, I did not know the Bible, and so Jesus's words "whatever you did for one of the least of these brothers of mine you did for me" (NIV) were very interesting indeed, for he had shown me what those words meant.

My family noticed the difference in me, for I was happier instead of being long-suffering, and I had lost the anger that I had used to always feel. Just about everything in life had a different purpose and a different priority now. I was nice to people in order to please God, not just to make myself seem loveable.

My personal problems didn't all stop right there and then, and I still had inward dragons to fight, but now I know that I am not alone in my struggles. I know that there is someone who feels my problems and understands where they come from, and who can help me through them all.

Merrie Gresham is the wife of Douglas Gresham, stepson of C. S. Lewis. In 1993 the couple moved from a farm in Tasmania to Leighlinbridge, County Carlow, Ireland, where they started Rathvinden Ministries, a retreat center for those in need of spiritual and emotional healing. The Greshams currently reside on the Mediterranean island of Malta.

29

Joy Was His Name

Melissa Kapp Hawkins

The theater company commune was empty for the first time since I'd been in Hungary. I seized the opportunity to work on my role in a large puppet workshop. I brought into the room all the materials I thought I would need, including the folder of resources I had packed for my first professional acting job. I had just earned my degree in acting and had been offered a position in a theater in Budapest. I could think of no offer more intriguing, more romantic, or better suited to my commitment to a life of autonomy and adventure above all else, so I accepted on the spot.

My family in Chicago did their best to feign excitement, but I'm sure they could not imagine how God would reach me in Budapest. I had spent the last ten years in bitter opposition to God, despite my family's endless attempts to woo and to frighten me towards him. If I were on the other side of the earth, who would be there to continue their efforts?

In order to understand the event that was about to happen in that workshop, it is important to know the condition of my heart. There was a precise moment in my early adolescence when I *chose* wrong. Although I was a missionary kid, I simply decided one day that I no longer accepted that title. I deliberately sabotaged my reputation and embraced every choice that would distinguish me from my family. This certainly meant specific lifestyle changes, but it was also a very conscious spiritual rebellion. I initially believed that I could break cleanly and completely away from their way of interpreting the world. I dabbled in witchcraft until I realized that it fit perfectly within their beliefs—that I had simply gone to the *other* side. I was not out to casually oppose them. I wanted true freedom from them.

Now, sitting in Budapest, I began to read through the folder, curious to see what papers I had deemed worthy of my suitcase. The first gem was a paper I had been asked to write in college on the subject of joy, an emotion which I was particularly poor at expressing. Pain, fear, and rage I could do; I was horrible at joy. My professor was appalled and demanded that I write a paper—the one now in my hands—explaining why I was so inept at joy. As I read what I had written, I laughed at the excuses I had offered, and I tossed it aside.

Next I discovered something in the folder that was entirely out of place. For years my sister had attempted to get me to read a particular book. She felt that I would identify somehow with the characters; for that reason alone, I was not about to read it. She bought me several copies, and after I "lost" each one, she began photocopying sections and writing comments in the margins. I had never taken the time to read a single word, but now, miles from home and painfully homesick, I felt terrible guilt as I looked at her handwriting. I will never know how those photocopies found their way into my folder, but I could not ignore once again the efforts of a sister I so dearly missed.

And so I began to read these carefully chosen pages from C. S. Lewis's *Surprised by Joy*. He described three beautiful moments from his childhood, explaining that they represented Joy, which operates like a kind of pain or grief that we want but that we never have the power to attain. I continued reading in dismay. He described the death of his mother, which was the turning point in his childhood. When his mother died, Lewis lost all security and reliable happiness in his life.

I could feel myself melting as I read these words, and I was furious. I had succeeded in holding God at bay for ten years, but now suddenly I felt him bursting into the room, uninvited. His name had not appeared once in those pages, and yet I knew more clearly than ever before that Joy was his name. I also knew how dangerous this was—how appealing God could be. I had never let him get this close before, but he wasn't providing any escape. I had been led to believe that my conversion would be my decision. I was wrong. Although I didn't go without a fight, that day there was no avoiding him.

After two hours of what felt like a great sea battle, during which I could not even utter his name, I finally took on water and sank. A blubbering mess on the floor, I spoke for the first time, saying, "I'm so tired" over and over and over again.

I woke the next morning with a start. What was I now? What did this mean for the rest of my life? Would God take my acting ambitions away? Would everyone laugh? How had I let this happen? I was sure this was the end of everything I loved, but I couldn't imagine him being out of my life ever again.

It was suddenly clear to me that during those ten years of rebellion, I had deliberately been keeping Joy from my life. I had been walking down the street figuratively forcing myself to stare at the sidewalk, terrified that I might catch an undeniable glimpse of the sky.

I received my first phone call from the States that day. It was my sister. After stumbling through the petty details of my life in Budapest, I finally exclaimed that I had something much more important to tell her. I began to recount the event. There was much weeping and laughter on both ends of the phone. She wasted little time before asking when this had happened. I told her when, exactly, and she went silent.

Two nights before, she told me, she had awakened in the middle of the night, unable to go back to sleep. She finally asked God what he woke her for, and his clear answer was to pray for me. We determined that this was precisely when I picked up those pages from C. S. Lewis on the other side of the world.

I asked her what to do next. I begged her to send one more copy of that book—immediately. But I also feared that the robustness of my family's long-established faith would flood this new vacuum, and I would forfeit the integrity and personal nature of my own encounter with God. And Jesus was not involved yet. The last thing I wanted to do was rush into a familiar religion simply to settle my new faith somewhere. My sister removed all pressure and encouraged me to let God woo me, slowly and precisely.

What followed was the most unexpected romance with God. In *Surprised by Joy* Lewis says, "The hardness of God is kinder than the softness of men, and His compulsion is our liberation," and I found that it was true. It was like nothing I had feared. I devoured

Surprised by Joy, and while it marks one of my most spiritual literary experiences, it was no road map to Christianity. Lewis, too, embraced theism before a more specific faith came into focus. He did, however, present a tremendous argument for the validity of the Bible, enough so that I found the courage one day to open it, and—despite my skepticism—in those pages I met my God.

While living in Hungary, I developed a friendship with a Hungarian pastor. During a long walk with him one day, I admitted that since my conversion I had lost my passion for theater. Everything else was falling away, even the things I wanted to hold on to. He staunchly declared that we were to have no passions, no pleasures, except those that we received through Jesus. I was a little stunned by what sounded like fundamentalism. And then, suddenly, I understood. The theater I was creating was not given to me by God, and consequently, it was meaningless. I would only regain my passion for theater when it was joined with that "far superior and endlessly echoing passion for God." It was such a simple discovery, but I could hardly contain myself—such joy!

When I got home that day I stumbled upon a quote from *The Jesus I Never Knew* by Philip Yancey: "The Lord Jesus who rules my life is not a sentimental, self-pitying weakling. He was a Jew, a carpenter, and strong. He took into his own heart, for our sakes, that pain which brings 'wisdom through the awful grace of God.'" All at once I realized that I was speaking of Jesus as a reality. I was using his name as though I had met him. I could not prove that Jesus was real that night, but I could acknowledge his indispensable role—God Incarnate. The apostle Paul boldly called Jesus "the image of the invisible God. . . . For God was pleased to have all his fullness dwell in him" (Col. 1:15, 19 NIV). I was convinced.

As I lost everything, he replaced it or gave it back tenfold. The first addiction I had to confront was, in fact, theater. God wanted to know if I could regain my enthusiasm for acting if he asked me to. The minute I acknowledged that I could, he commissioned me to do the most captivating piece of theater I've ever come across. It was literally dropped into my lap by a missionary opera singer in Budapest. After I read it, I set out to meet the playwright, the first person I found who had successfully married faith and art and compromised neither. I crossed a total of four borders without a valid visa in order to meet him. I was sure that God would part the waters for me to meet this individual.

I spent one of the most memorable weeks of my life in Transylvania with the Visky family, during which the playwright gave me the rights to the English premiere of the one-woman show. It was my first assignment from God, and although it took three years, it finally opened in the summer of 2006. Andras Visky's *Juliet: A Dialogue about Love* began an international tour in 2007, already having been performed in Budapest and Transylvania. I look forward to a long collaboration with Andras Visky.

Melissa Kapp Hawkins lives in the Chicago suburbs with her husband, Eric, and six-year-old son, Korbin. Visit her website at www.juliet-tour.com.

30

Heart of a Rebel

LIZ CURTIS HIGGS

Fallen man is not simply an imperfect creature who needs improvement: he is a rebel who must lay down his arms. —C. S. Lewis, *Mere Christianity*

February 1982. The ceilings were high, the windows drafty, and the heat in my century-old apartment house was little more than a rumor. Curled up in a sagging club chair, intently reading, I hardly noticed the midwinter cold, warmed as I was by the words before me and the late-afternoon sun pouring through the long, narrow windows of my study.

"Read this book," two friends had urged me. Because I'd grown to love and respect them, and because the title intrigued me, I purchased *Mere Christianity* and began, as all serious readers do, with the preface: "The contents of this book were first given on the air . . ." Well, now. Hooked from the very start. Hadn't I spent the last five years working as a radio broadcaster? I burrowed deeper into my faded chintz cushions and kept reading, intrigued by the writer's strong sense of who he was and who he was not. "I am a very ordinary layman of the Church of England, not especially 'high,' nor especially 'low,' nor especially anything else." Odd. My friends had insisted he was a genius. Three pages into the book, humble seemed a much better fit.

I knew nothing of Lewis's work or reputation. Perhaps that was for the best. I came to Lewis without my defensive shield at the ready. Even had I been prepared, the honesty of his words would have disarmed me: "There are questions at issue between Christians to which I do not think we have been told the answer." Uh-oh. I had nothing but questions—questions about the existence of God, the validity of faith, the necessity of church. Such things mattered a great deal to my two friends, which bewildered me. Intelligent, talented, well-read, much-traveled people, yet they were genuinely enthusiastic about going to church. How was that possible?

"Read this . . ."

And so I kept reading, all through the wintry afternoon. There was no denying this Lewis guy had me pegged: a disillusioned young woman of twenty-seven who'd gotten turned off by denominational infighting and hypocritical churchgoers. At least that's what I told people. Fear was the real reason: fear that I'd gone too far, done too much. Fear that, if God was real, I'd blown it, big time. Enter Lewis, a middle-aged Irish male, a scholar and a soldier, who put into words the deepest longings of my soul: "There is something, or a Someone, who against all divergences of belief, all differences of temperament, all memories of mutual persecution, speaks with the same voice." When had I stopped listening? And would that voice still speak to me, after all I'd done? All the men, all the drugs, all the booze, all the lies—after all that, would the Someone I once called God the Father care about his long-lost daughter?

I kept reading, pulled from one paragraph to the next by Lewis's clarity of thought and ironclad logic. Within five pages he'd not only convinced me that Right and Wrong existed—me, the queen of loosey-goosey, do-what-feels-good relativism!—he'd also assured me that none of us was any good at keeping that sacred law. Ouch. Even worse, Lewis stated that when we stumbled, we invariably shifted the responsibility for our failures elsewhere and conjured up flimsy excuses. "It is only our bad temper that we put down to being tired or worried or hungry; we put our good temper down to ourselves." Ouch again.

Tempted as I might have been to toss the book against the wall at such bold claims, I couldn't bring myself to do so because his arguments were irrefutable: I did know Right from Wrong. Although I'd spent ten years convincing myself that I enjoyed being a bad girl, the ugly truth was, I hated it. Living at the bottom of a dark pit had grown lonelier with each passing year. Shocking people with my edgy lifestyle had lost its appeal. The term paper from my sophomore year of college—"Why I Don't Believe in God"—suddenly felt like blasphemy.

Chastised, I continued reading, certain that after he built a strong case against my moral failures, Lewis would offer a ray of hope. He seemed genuinely concerned that I understood what was at stake. Nothing short of eternity; nothing less than everything. Surely he wouldn't quit before giving me some good news, some way of escape. He was leading up to a critical conclusion, that much was clear. Something monumental. Undeniable. Change was in the air, tangible as the dust motes in my study.

Page by page he'd escorted me—and millions of other readers over the last sixty years—a thousand miles, from not believing in God to agreeing that God exists. Right there in my armchair, within easy reach of a toasted-cheese sandwich and a cold beer. I'd been guided by a benevolent stranger over the dividing wall between belief in nothing to belief in Something. He'd done it with nothing but words on a page, spilling nary a drop of blood on my study floor.

How does a writer like C. S. Lewis manage such a feat? With great care and by the power of the Holy Spirit. He invites us to examine our own lives and see if we agree with his assessments.

Lewis is not for the casual reader, nor is *Mere Christianity* meant to be read in a single sitting. That February long ago I allowed his dangerous words to sink in, first one evening and then the next, reading with a mix of dread and anticipation as he described "the thing we most need and the thing we most want to hide from." I'd been hiding from God for a decade. Lewis and I spent the week together—he on the printed page, I in my armchair—wrestling demons of doubt and despair. More than once, he made me laugh: "When you are arguing against Him you are arguing against the very power that makes you able to argue at all: it is like cutting off the branch you are sitting on." Ha, ha, ha. Chainsaw, please.

He didn't mince words, stating in no uncertain terms that Christ did "not come to torment your natural self, but to kill it." I was a product of the self-indulgent '60s, honed by the feminism of the '70s. Kill my natural self? Humph. This God of his was expecting a lot.

And yet . . . each time my temper notched up a degree, Lewis would touch a cool drop of water to my lips: "When you come to knowing God, the initiative lies on His side." Oh. I wasn't expected to manage things on my own, then. Assuaged once again, I kept reading.

The fact that Lewis invites, even applauds, differences of opinion says a great deal about his confidence in his beliefs and his focus on the central issue of Christianity, the Mere of the book's title. How simply that core truth is stated: "Now, today, this moment, is our chance to choose the right side." And how cunningly we avoid such surrender, to which Lewis warns, "If you are contented with simply being nice, you are still a rebel." That was me back then, rebellious to the core. On many days, that still is me. Chafing against God's will for me, preferring my own carefully plotted calendar. Daily I have to lay down my rebel's weaponry and embrace the eternal truth, eloquently stated by Lewis in the final pages: "The more we get what we now call 'ourselves' out of the way and let Him take us over, the more truly ourselves we become."

And are you wondering what became of that young rebel, reading C. S. Lewis in her drafty apartment many Februarys ago? On a Sabbath evening, I closed Lewis's book in stunned silence, only one thought left banging around in my head: If a man that brilliant, that educated, that seasoned by love and war, believed with all his heart and mind that "there is one God and that Jesus Christ is His only Son," then who was I to argue with such a man?

So I did not argue. Nor did I stop with Lewis, turning instead to a more seminal work. Seated at an old maple table rescued from my mother's attic, I opened my Bible to the book of Romans (also recommended reading from my helpful friends) and soon found Romans 5:8: "But God demonstrates His own love toward us, in that while we were yet sinners, Christ died for us" (NASB).

This rebel's heart was finally and completely undone. My forehead fell onto the pages, and I drenched them with my tears. Sorrow and joy flowed, mingled down. Deep inside me, the truth beat like a drum: I was a sinner. I was loved. And I was forgiven.

Liz Curtis Higgs is the author of twenty-six books for adults and children. She spent ten years in broadcasting before her writing and public speaking career. Some of her best-selling books include *Bad Girls of the Bible*, *Really Bad Girls of the Bible*, and *Unveiling Mary Magdalene*. Her award-winning children's books include *The Pumpkin Patch Parable* and *The Parable of the Lily*. Liz and her husband, Bill, live in a nineteenth-century farmhouse in Louisville, Kentucky.

31

My Original Encounter with C. S. Lewis

Walter Hooper

My favorite year was 1953. I was a senior at the University of North Carolina at Chapel Hill, and while that happy life was threatened by the Korean War, when every young man my age was being drafted, this made the few remaining months all the sweeter. The draft board promised to leave me alone until I could complete my degree at Christmas. And so I made the most of the fall term of 1953.

I belonged to a Bible study group that met in my dormitory. Although I was a member of the soccer team, everyone knew that the real heroes of the university were the football players. I regarded myself as very fortunate, for I knew the captain of the football team, George Norris. He led our Bible study, and he was the most spiritually mature person I knew. He and I were also members of InterVarsity Christian Fellowship, which was well represented at the university.

But more important than anything, George Norris was the first person I heard mention C. S. Lewis. I recall him saying something about *The Screwtape Letters*, but I didn't come across that work until later. What George introduced me to was a book very popular in Chapel Hill at the time, J. B. Phillips's *Letters to Young Churches: A Translation of the New Testament Epistles* with an introduction by C. S. Lewis.

Those who can go into a bookshop today and wonder which of twenty or thirty Lewis titles to buy can hardly imagine what it was like to those three or four of us in Chapel Hill who sensed the greatness of this man from having read a page or so of his writings. In any event, I will forever be grateful to George Norris for introducing me to J. B. Phillips's translation of the New Testament Epistles—with its introduction by C. S. Lewis. Will you think me a fool if I tell you that, all these years later, that piece of writing is *still* making a conquest of me? I remember where I was sitting when I read it, and I recollect its effect on me as if it happened yesterday. What did Lewis *say* that was so earthshaking? That's just the point. Nothing he said was particularly unusual. The difference, apart from his extraordinary lucidity and beautifully phrased paragraphs, was that he was *sure* of what he said. That certainty was combined with an ability to express profound things in everyday English. Writing about the everyday Greek that the New Testament was originally written in, he said: "The same divine humility which decreed that God should become a baby at a peasant-woman's breast, and later an arrested field-preacher in the hands of the Roman police, decreed also that He should be preached in a vulgar, prosaic and unliterary language."

His voice was different from any I'd ever heard before. When I mentioned how greatly I was affected by Lewis to my friends in 1953, they asked me what it was about Lewis that did this. I said, "This man *really* believes!" One of them replied, "But don't most Christians 'really' believe?" "Not like Lewis!" I said. What came through that introduction was not simply information about the Epistles, but something about *Lewis*. I knew I'd stumbled upon someone whose faith was as certain as that of the apostles. I remember thinking at the time, *This man makes it sound as if the events recorded in the New Testament took place about five minutes ago, and are as important* now *as they were then*. Lewis believed, it seemed to me, with the certainty of those who had been with Jesus. Was there more of such writing?

I was soon busy preparing for exams, but I nevertheless searched the bookshops of Chapel Hill for anything by Lewis. I could find nothing. My home was in Reidsville, North Carolina, and I continued the search in nearby Greensboro. There I came across Straughn's Bookshop, run by the two elderly Straughn sisters. They liked to put the right book in the right hands, and they told me not to worry, that they would send me whatever books they could find by C. S. Lewis.

As it turned out, they found Lewis's *Miracles: A Preliminary Study* on the eve of my departure for Fort Jackson, South Carolina, the first week of January 1954. I was able to sample it on the bus ride to Fort Jackson. After I got there, the problem was knowing what to do with the book, because I went straight into basic training. I didn't worry about this long because I could not bear to be parted from this book, and during nearly the whole of basic training—eight weeks—it was under my shirt.

Of course, I would have liked to have read *Miracles* in bed at night, when, that is, we were finally allowed to go there. Unfortunately, the officers knew that if we so much as sat on our bunks, we'd fall asleep. So the rule was that no one could lie, or even sit, on his bed until 11:30 p.m. Having been up since 4:30 a.m., we could not possibly stay awake once we touched our beds. So reading had to be fitted into daylight hours.

Basic training consisted of fifty-minute periods of rifle training, bayonet practice, climbing under barbed wire, firing bazookas, and throwing grenades. After each session there was a ten-minute cigarette break. The moment bayonet practice or whatever it was ended, I sat under the pine trees and read *Miracles*. It meant breaking off in mid-sentence when we were ordered to do whatever was next on the schedule, but even a quick dip into a book by Lewis is different from reading anything else. Then came a problem. We began calisthenics. What was I to do with *Miracles* while jumping up and down? The same thing I did while climbing under barbed wire—I kept the book in my shirt. How well I remember seeing that heavy book flying about under my green fatigue shirt as we did calisthenics. I expected any second that the sergeant would spot what was happening. By the grace of God—no one noticed!

And so amidst a thousand distractions, I read, page by page, my first book by C. S. Lewis. It remains in my memory as the greatest literary and theological experience of my life. I was savoring for the first time arguments about naturalism and supernaturalism, about miracles, about the doctrines of the incarnation and the resurrection. One of the most unforgettable moments of my life occurred under those pine trees at Fort Jackson when I came across Lewis's distinction between science and Christianity. I think I probably yelled out loud when I read in chapter 14 of *Miracles* "In science we have been reading only the notes to a poem; in Christianity we find the poem itself."

Why has no one told *me these things?* I asked myself many times. Had they tried to and found me inattentive? No: I *knew* I'd never read anything like this. Indeed, had I not had this firsthand experience, I would not have believed it possible for anyone to express such deep truths in language of such brilliant clarity. Besides this, anyone who has read even a few pages of almost any work by Lewis will know what a depth of knowledge he wrote from. One of the many pleasures of *Miracles* was becoming familiar with "the furniture" of Lewis's mind—the incomparable Judeo-Christian background which includes such riches as Dante, Boethius, the gardens of the Hesperides, Adonis, Osiris, and Plato. I had entered the world of C. S. Lewis, and I had no idea at the time how much better it would get.

Walter Hooper is the literary adviser to the estate of C. S. Lewis, author of *C. S. Lewis: A Complete Guide to His Life and Works*, and editor of the three volumes of *The Collected Letters of C. S. Lewis*, among other writings, such as the forewords to many books about Lewis, including this one. Just before Lewis's death in 1963, he served as his private secretary, later devoting himself to Lewis's memory. Walter Hooper lives in Oxford, England.

32

We All Have the Same Difficulty

Thomas Howard

We all have the same difficulty here: how to tap into some shape the great heap of debts we owe to C. S. Lewis. There are, by now, millions of us.

I first came upon his name when an older sister of mine came home from college with a book that had been required in a course she was taking and pressed it on me. I was about twelve at the time. But how odd it was—these letters from a seasoned old demon to a fledgling devil on how to leach away the faith of a Christian. I was galvanized, of course, but the author's name meant nothing to me (he wasn't one of the great Bible teachers who held the limelight in those palmy 1940s days of Philadelphia fundamentalism). Who he might be, no one could say, but what he wrote sounded as though he might be a Christian, so that was all right.

My next encounter with this man's *oeuvre* (as they used to say in English departments) occurred in a course in philosophical apologetics at Wheaton College in Illinois, where we were required to read *Miracles*, *Mere Christianity*, and I think *The Abolition of Man*. A man called Kenneth Kantzer was the professor, and I owe him a great debt for putting Lewis in front of us all.

But this is an essay, not about Lewis and all of his books generally, but about Lewis as a spiritual mentor.

Perhaps the most apposite thing to be said here is that *all* of his books, I think, have helped form me in the faith, even such unlikely works as *The Discarded Image*, *The Allegory of Love*, and *English Literature in the Sixteenth Century Excluding Drama*. Certainly I would wish to include here *A Preface to "Paradise Lost."* The thing about all of these works is that, whether or not the topic at hand appears to be at all "spiritual," one nevertheless finds oneself in any of his books faced with something brisk, energetic, clean, and robust, as opposed to the earnest, swampy, and eager literature, written in terrible English prose, that fills religious bookstores in our own epoch. Lewis's sturdy, searching, and hearty way of addressing any topic cannot help but have its effect on one's own habits of thought, and hence in one's prayers and self-examination.

I, like everyone else, have found such volumes as *Letters to Malcolm*, *Reflections on the Psalms*, and *The Problem of Pain* to be almost incalculably formative. Again, it is the voice speaking as much as the points made that finds its way into one's inner being.

There is no question about it—Lewis has been a spiritual mentor to me (although he would, I think, have jibbed mightily at the term) through his imaginative works. It is as though the entire universe has been unfurled and one has been vouchsafed a glimpse of glory and of the whole panoply of holiness. "Who can tell the pleasure, who recount the treasure" (to quote the hymn) that one stumbles upon in these works. Reepicheep: great pluck, fathomless courtesy, purity of heart, zeal for the right. Puddleglum: damp, melancholy, unlikely, but a hero in making his own flesh a burnt sacrifice for the salvation of others. Mr. and Mrs. Beaver: simple, unimportant, utterly unprepossessing, but generous, courageous, cheerful, and waiting for the consolation of Israel. Frank the Cabbie: only a London cabbie—but *good* (to his customers, to his wife, and to his horse) and therefore granted the Beatific Vision. Jewel the Unicorn, whose fragrance, delicacy, and beauty lances our hearts with yearning for those unimaginable precincts from which he hails. Ransom, the self-effacing don asked to be the savior of a whole world. But then also Edmund and Eustace Clarence Scrubb: tiresome, odious little creatures, saved from ruin by grace and transfigured into noble men. Weston and Wither, Frost, Straik, Filostrato, Fairy Hardcastle, and the whole Belbury meinie: icons from hell. And Jane and Mark Studdock, both shackled in awful vanity, with a marriage in desperate straits; and then Jane rescued and remade at St. Anne's, which is a minuscule appearance of Logres (which Lewis got from Charles Williams), and Mark saved in the nick of time by Jane saying to herself that it was "high time" someone went down through the garden, past the piggeries, and looked after the poor sod.

Who can read all of this and not himself be bidden to the gates of holiness? God (literally—certainly not I) only knows what I owe to Lewis here.

I visited Lewis at The Kilns in 1963 and ventured, timorously, that my favorite of his books was *Till We Have Faces*. Fancy my delight when he agreed that it was his. The tale of Orual captivated me. From the opening . . . Glome, to the closing where Orual, finally exhausted with her quarrel with the gods, is overcome by sheer Joy. Lewis has written as rich and complex a rendition of the myth of Cupid and Psyche as that story has ever had.

I cannot write about all of this without the tears starting into my eyes. That, perhaps, as well as anything, speaks of my debt to Lewis as a spiritual mentor.

Highly regarded as an authority on the fiction of C. S. Lewis and Charles Williams, **Thomas Howard** has taught English and literature for over thirty years. He is the author of *The Achievement of C. S. Lewis*, *Narnia and Beyond*, *The Novels of Charles Williams*, and many other books. He and his wife, Lovelace, live in Manchester, Massachusetts.

33

My Life Has Never Been the Same

Richard James

An old proverb says that "Some people come into our lives and quickly go, but others stay awhile and leave footprints on our hearts, and we are never the same." In regards to C. S. Lewis—Oxford don, Cambridge professor, Christian author, and literary critic—that old adage has proved itself to be true in my life. During my first year as a student at the University of Virginia, I found myself facing some serious doubts about my faith, and a friend suggested that I read *Mere Christianity* by C. S. Lewis. There I found clarity, logic, and some answers for my questions of faith. There I also discovered that I did not have to be afraid of facing the questions that were being posed to me by fellow students and professors. Reading that book was a turning point in my life as I learned that being a Christian meant not only loving God with all of my heart but also loving him with my entire mind.

Who would have imagined that that advice, given over forty years ago, would have had such an indelible influence upon my life? After I read *Mere Christianity*, I then read *The Screwtape Letters*. How creative and how practical this book was as it helped me see myself, and the temptations and trials I faced, with both new insight and humor. Over the next several months came *The Problem of Pain*,

Miracles, *Reflections on the Psalms*, *The Abolition of Man*, *The Four Loves*, *Surprised by Joy*, and *A Grief Observed*. Each one of these was foundational in helping me see my faith with new vision. I have read each one several times, discovering for myself that, second only to the New Testament, Lewis's devotional, biographical, and apologetical works have played a significant role in guiding me to a closer walk with Jesus Christ. They were also an important resource for me in my early ministry at the small Christian church where I served during my last two years of college. In addition, when I again faced several intellectual questions in seminary, these same books, especially *Miracles*, helped me sort through much of the liberal antisupernatural assumptions I found in many of my classes.

While in college, I tried to read some of Lewis's other fiction besides *The Screwtape Letters*, such as *The Great Divorce* and the Space Trilogy, but after a few chapters of each book I seemed to lose interest. All four books would sit on my bookshelf for several more years before I was drawn back to them with fresh interest.

Following my graduation from college, I married and then moved to Lexington, Kentucky, to attend seminary. It was there, in 1969, while participating in a Christian coffeehouse ministry, that I first heard several of the Chronicles of Narnia books read as part of the ministry to the young people whom we were trying to reach with the gospel. While still deeply spiritual, these books showed me an aspect of Lewis that I had not yet experienced. The wonder, the joy, the adventure, the awe-filled experience with Aslan in Narnia—all of these gave me a fresh vision of what the Christian life could really be like in our own world. I bought all seven of those books and, beginning with *The Lion, the Witch and the Wardrobe*, my wife and I read them to each other at night before we went to bed. So significant in our relationship was this fresh spiritual experience with the Chronicles of Narnia that three years later we named our first son David Edmund after Edmund, the boy for whom Aslan had died in *The Lion, the Witch and the Wardrobe*.

But something else also followed the reading of these Narnian stories. I developed a renewed interest in reading some of Lewis's other fiction that I had at first rejected—*The Great Divorce* and those Space Trilogy stories. Plus, I eventually found and read *The Pilgrim's Regress* and *Till We Have Faces*. I especially enjoyed reading *Perelandra*'s mythic retelling of the Garden of Eden story—how Ransom faithfully fulfilled his mission in assisting the Green Lady to overcome the temptations she confronted as that planet's Eve. For several years it was my favorite work of fiction by Lewis.

Having access to an excellent theological library in seminary, I broadened my knowledge of Lewis's writings when I discovered several smaller books of essays, including *The Weight of Glory*, *The World's Last Night*, and *Christian Reflections*, along with the much-larger collection, *God in the Dock*. I bought these books, and whenever I had a few extra minutes, I enjoyed delving into Lewis's thoughts on the many ethical, theological, and cultural concerns of his day. Each of these, along with the already-mentioned theological and devotional materials, gave a depth and breadth to my maturing faith in Christ. I was often amazed at how Lewis as an educated layman had stood so firm in his own faith and had been able to share that "mere Christianity" so cogently with others.

While in college, I read about Lewis's early life and his conversion in *Surprised by Joy*; a few years later, in the seminary library, I came across Chad Walsh's *C. S. Lewis: Apostle to the Skeptics*. This was the first of many biographies of Lewis that I have read, and in them all I have found that if God could use a somewhat-flawed instrument like Lewis to bring many to Christ, then maybe he could also use me.

My devotion to Lewis through the years has led me to many conferences, to Lewis societies, and to the marvelous Marion E. Wade Center, which houses a collection of materials by and about Lewis and six other like-minded writers. These others, too, have nourished my soul so that, through Lewis, I have received spiritual mentorship at the faithful hands of others.

All in all, as I look back over the more than forty years of contact with C. S. Lewis and his writings, it has made my faith in Jesus Christ stronger and deeper with its focus on mere Christianity, and it has also made me both a more critical and imaginative thinker and a better-informed person, especially about the Western literary heritage. Like all of us, Lewis's feet were made of clay, and he had many faults. But in spite of his flaws, I continue to be blessed by his writings and by others who have studied his works. And thus, through both his life and his words, C. S. Lewis has left his footprints deeply upon my heart, and my life has never been the same. May it also be so for any who read these words.

A graduate of the University of Virginia (B.A. in history) and Lexington Theological Seminary (M.Div.), **Richard James** serves as pastor of the First Christian Church in Albany, Kentucky. A contributor to the *C. S. Lewis Readers' Encyclopedia*, James lectures widely on Lewis and edits The Cumberland River Lamp Post, a website for articles and sermons relating to C. S. Lewis. He and his wife, Mary, have three children.

34

He Shaped My Mind

David Lyle Jeffrey

When I entered Wheaton College as a seventeen-year-old freshman, I had not heard of C. S. Lewis, much less read him. During the next two years I heard of him, but I read only *The Screwtape Letters*. But in my junior year, in a course with Dr. Clyde S. Kilby, I read the Space Trilogy, *Till We Have Faces*, many of Lewis's essays and works of lay theology, and, of course, *Mere Christianity* and *Surprised by Joy*. During the same semester, I read some of the Narnia Chronicles to the children I was babysitting and reread *The Weight of Glory*. It was an exhilarating, theologically revolutionary semester. Like many a student of my day, I was affected by Lewis at levels deeper than I could yet fathom. It would take years for me to swim in such waters.

Dr. Kilby had already talked to me in early autumn about the possibility of my applying to study with Lewis at Magdalene College, Cambridge, for a doctorate in philosophy. Lewis died before the term was out, on the same day as President John F. Kennedy, although I did not learn of Lewis's death till two weeks later. The next spring two of my classmates, who recognized how deeply Lewis's essays had affected me, asked if I imagined myself trying to write like Lewis and for similar lay-theological purposes. I firmly demurred. We were standing on the south steps of the old student union building, and I can remember one of them pressing the point: "What is the most important thing you have gotten out of Lewis?"

I remember answering, far too confidently, that what I had mostly learned is that in the humane disciplines, one has so much learning to absorb that one's best work only starts to emerge about the age of fifty-five. I added that what I most aspired to do myself was not to write *about* Lewis but rather to read the books that had made him such a richly furbished Christian thinker.

I had set myself a tall order, and at sixty-five now, I haven't yet filled it. But I did eventually become a medievalist at Princeton, studying under Lewis's American rival, D. W. Robertson Jr., and I read voluminously along lines that I felt Lewis not only would have recognized but even approved.

But Lewis was far from done with me. Later in graduate school I read *A Preface to "Paradise Lost," The Discarded Image*, *Studies in Words* (a mesmerizing gem of a book), and *English Literature in the Sixteenth Century Excluding Drama*. I also read *Reflections on the Psalms*—at the time almost as disappointing to me as Lewis's poetry. *The Discarded Image* and *Studies in Words* I found formative, sending me deeper into their subject matter. Now his poems, perhaps especially his "The Apologist's Evening Prayer," have on many occasions prompted an examination of conscience in me, as well as providing for spiritually enriching reflection. But the book that was to galvanize my approach to the teaching of literature I would not open for another decade.

An Experiment in Criticism is now for me the signature book by Lewis, the one I require of my own students *almost* as though it is a kind of handbook to the gospel. In this book Lewis declares his principles regarding reading itself, which for him is the birthplace and nursemaid of all intellectual life.

In his distinction between the professionally driven reader and the "literary" reader, I have found almost everything necessary to instruct students in respect of the *raison d'être* of literary study—indeed of higher learning in the humanities. *Experiment* is a work of discerning, clarifying genius; in its stark distinctions and affectionate elevation of the life of the imaginative mind, this book seems to me to distill the very essence of Lewis's approach to every text and every truth he loved. For this slim volume, which I wish had come to me first rather than last among the writings of Lewis, I shall be always grateful. *An*

Experiment in Criticism, more than any other influence, has shaped my mind to the task of teaching literature, and it remains the one book by Lewis by which I would most like my own work to be marked.

David Lyle Jeffrey, Distinguished Professor of Literature and the Humanities at Baylor University, Waco, Texas, has also served as department chair at both the University of Ottawa and the University of Victoria and as a guest professor at Beijing University. Jeffrey is the author of numerous books, including *A Dictionary of Biblical Tradition in English Literature* (1992) and *Houses of the Interpreter* (2003). His current research interests involve the relationship of biblical humanities to literary and artistic expression. He and his wife live in Waco, Texas.

35

No Possible Rebuttal

Dorothy Karabin

A good deal of my young life was spent rejecting a God who I felt was uncaring, harsh, and punitive—if he existed at all. "I fled Him, down the nights and down the days; / I fled Him, down the arches of the years," as Francis Thompson so eloquently put it. My childhood had been scarred by abuse, anxiety, and repression, all the while intermingled with an almost-fanatical, forced attention to God and religion. My subsequent reaction to this as I reached maturity and achieved independence was one of barely suppressed anger and bitterness as I vehemently rejected what I considered to be purely nonsense. This, sad to say, kept me from any knowledge of God's love and forgiveness. I had effectively closed the door to him.

God gave me a lot of time to cool off before he confronted me with my colossal pride. It was in October of 1977 when I was fifty-three years of age that he finally dealt with me, up front and personal, you might say. I was at home from work with a nasty cold; with time hanging heavily on my hands, I looked for something to read. My son, Brian, a sophomore at Northern Illinois University, had brought home *Mere Christianity* and had suggested that I read it, which, of course, I diligently avoided. But on that fateful day I picked it up and began to read. I read with increasing interest, intrigued by Lewis's simple but profound discussion of morality. This was not entirely new to me, but I was seeing it in a different light.

I came to chapter 8, "The Great Sin." By the time I finished it, I was totally devastated. I was seeing myself for the first time as God saw me—a flagrant sinner—and the chasm between him and me was vast. I saw through all my previous, pitiful defenses in which God had become the scapegoat for my miserable childhood. Alternating between sobbing on my knees and pacing the room, I was in utter despair. My completely "anti-God state of mind" as Lewis called it, shattered my pride into a million pieces.

As I calmed down somewhat, I became aware of a presence in the room with me which was warm, serene, and somehow inviting. The thought came into my mind that I had to do something. To escape from my state of despair, I had to get help. Getting out the telephone directory, I looked for the number of a church located a few blocks away. That is when I became aware of a second presence in the room with me, more insistent and more demanding that I not make that call. A fierce battle ensued, which lasted for hours. I was torn between what I wanted to do and yet could not do. No words were spoken aloud except my repeated "I will do it," but the clamor in my head was deafening. Thankfully, God's grace kept me resolute, because, frankly, I was no match for the powers of darkness. I finally made the call and later saw the minister. Listening to him read chapters seven and eight from the book of Romans was a deep revelation to me.

However, my spiritual journey was not a sudden *fait accompli*. I was to spend the next year on my knees through sleepless nights, crying out for God's mercy to sustain me as my fallen nature struggled for control. I lived with the New Testament, and the words of Christ fed me constantly. I read all of Lewis's books I could find, and they were very helpful.

During that time there were incidents that happened which were certainly otherworldly. I cannot say it any other way. I am reluctant to assign a definite meaning to them, because they could be construed as illogical or just happenstance, and so they would be to an unbeliever. It is only as you take the first step into faith that you begin to realize how loving, forgiving, and supporting God is. It makes the behavior of the father running to meet his prodigal son entirely credible.

I will always be grateful for C. S. Lewis and his writings. I have since read many other books that present the Christian message, but

I seriously doubt that they would have had the same effect on me as *Mere Christianity* did at that time of my life. Lewis has a special gift, a way of putting a controversial topic before the reader that cannot be easily shrugged off. His examples to illustrate his points are sometimes disarming and witty, and sometimes extremely sharp, brooking no possible rebuttal.

During the time of my conversion, I felt compelled to write about my experiences. As I learned the things of God, I had to write about them, no doubt to fix them more firmly in my mind or to help clarify the confusion that surfaced in my thoughts from time to time. This compulsion waned over time, but reading these writings now makes me come away with a sense of the wonder of it all, that the majestic, all-powerful God would condescend to touch such an unrepentant sinner as I was.

Over the course of time the Spirit of God healed me of the effects of my sad childhood, and I was able to experience the joy and relief of forgiving those who had hurt me, even as God had forgiven me for having turned against him. I will always be filled with love and gratitude for my Lord and Savior.

One Saturday morning while visiting the Wade Center at Wheaton College, **Dorothy Karabin** volunteered that her life had been "turned around" after reading *Mere Christianity*. Born and raised in Chicago, Mrs. Karabin worked as a registered nurse when not raising her four children. She and her husband have seven grandchildren and live in Wheaton, Illinois.

36

A Mind Sharp as a Scalpel

Clyde S. Kilby's Encounter with C. S. Lewis

Mary Anne Phemister

Wheaton College English professor Clyde S. Kilby first discovered C. S. Lewis after purchasing *The Case for Christianity* at his college bookstore in the early 1940s. In *The Christian World of C. S. Lewis* Kilby says that he found in the writings of the Oxford don "a mind sharp as a scalpel and as intent as a surgeon upon the separation of the diseased from the healthy." Wanting to read more by this incisive author, Kilby searched out every book Lewis had written. He then began a correspondence with the man "who had won, inside and deep, a battle against pose, evasion, expedience, and the ever-so-little lie." That correspondence and the connection that subsequently arose between the two men had far-reaching echoes that still reverberate today.

In his introduction to *Images of Salvation in the Fiction of C. S. Lewis* Kilby wrote,

> I was overwhelmed by the powerful logic of works such as *Mere Christianity*, *Miracles*, and *The Problem of Pain*. I felt that no Christian I had ever read, unless it were G. K. Chesterton, had spoken so clearly or so cogently for Christianity. I belonged, as I still do, among conservative Christians, and in those days, when liberal theology seemed to be taking over the religious world, we were all seeking explicitly lucid and logical statements in defense of our faith. Lewis became our hero—at least he became mine.

Kilby was far from alone in finding in Lewis a champion for orthodox Christianity.

Professor Kilby readily admitted that he came to appreciate Lewis's fiction long after he found riches in his scholarly and apologetic works. Not that Kilby avoided fiction—after all, Kilby was a professor of English language and literature. He had learned that among young people in particular, a good story is more likely to make a lasting impression than merely theoretical presentations. Once he found that the charm would also work upon him, he soon "gobbled up the Narnia stories, recognizing that they belonged among the classics for children and were an equally golden gift for adults," including himself. In 1953, Kilby had the opportunity to visit Lewis in his rooms at Magdalen College, Oxford, cementing their epistolary friendship, which continued until Lewis's death in 1963. A friendship with the Lewis family continued through Kilby's correspondence with Lewis's brother Warren until the latter passed away in 1973.

His acquaintance with Lewis's work led Kilby to other British writers who had contributed to Lewis's imaginative and spiritual growth. In September 1964, nearly a year after Lewis's death, Kilby first met J. R. R. Tolkien. That relationship also bloomed into a literary friendship, culminating in Tolkien's solicitation of Kilby's assistance in getting *The Silmarillion* narratives sorted out and prepared for publication. In this way, Kilby assumed the role that Lewis had occupied when helping Tolkien to finish writing and to publish The Lord of the Rings. Tolkien wrote to Kilby that he needed "the actual *presence* of a friend and advisor at one's side." (For more about Kilby's encounters with Tolkien, see *Tolkien and the Silmarillion*, Harold Shaw Publishers, 1976.)

In the summer of 1965, while working with Tolkien, Kilby began to consider forming a collection of the books and letters of C. S. Lewis and his colleagues. Kilby could scarcely have imagined the expansive results of his seemingly simple idea. What began with a few books and fifteen letters of Kilby's correspondence with Lewis has expanded into the most comprehensive collection in the world of the letters, manuscripts, first editions, and primary and secondary materials of Lewis and six other British authors who were closely associated with him—J. R. R. Tolkien, G. K. Chesterton, George MacDonald, Owen Barfield, Dorothy L. Sayers, and Charles Williams. Dr. Kilby was soon to become one of America's foremost experts on the Inklings, that unofficial group often called the "Oxford Christians." This internationally recognized collection housed in the Marion E. Wade Center on the campus of Wheaton College regularly draws thousands of visitors and researchers from around the world.

After Lewis's death, Kilby became friends with Lewis's brother, Major Warren Lewis, called Warnie by his close acquaintances. Warnie got on so well with Kilby that he directed that his and his brother's papers be given to the Wheaton College collection after his death.

Notre Dame historian Mark Noll credits Clyde S. Kilby with being "the one who introduced Americans to Lewis, Tolkien, and Chesterton and to their bracing vision of God's creating grace." Noll recalls that while he was a student at Wheaton College, Kilby opened for him and many others "a wardrobe into a land of wonder where the Lion stalked." Before Noll took Kilby's course on the English Romantic poets, he admits that he had no idea who C. S. Lewis was, but recalls that "Kilby was not going to let anyone escape from his college without finding out." Noll surmises that after Billy Graham, Lewis was "the most important intellectual influence over the last thirty years on American evangelicals . . . and for many evangelicals, Kilby was the one who first made Lewis known" (*The Reformed Journal*, December 1986, p. 7). The Clyde S. Kilby Professorship in English Literature was established in his honor in 1982. Kilby found in Lewis a spiritual mentor worth following and proclaiming throughout his academic career, and Kilby's legacy, as a champion of Lewis, has led many down the same path.

Professor Clyde S. Kilby (1902–1986) authored a long list of books, many that center on the life and works of C. S. Lewis. These include *The Christian World of C. S. Lewis*, *C. S. Lewis: Images of His World* (with Douglas Gilbert), and *Images of Salvation in the Fiction of C. S. Lewis*. With Marjorie Lamp Mead he edited the diaries of Lewis's brother, Major Warren Hamilton Lewis, published as *Brothers and Friends: An Intimate Portrait of C. S. Lewis*.

37

A Writer We Can Read for the Rest of Our Lives

Don W. King

In the fall of 1971 I was a sophomore at Virginia Tech. Like many others, I had a job on campus to earn some spending money. For me this meant ten to fifteen hours a week washing dishes in one of the huge campus cafeterias. One day at the end of my shift someone walked up to me and gave me a tattered copy of *The Lion, the Witch and the Wardrobe*. I doubt that I had heard of C. S. Lewis before then; I certainly did not know him well. Since I was a literature major, I was always hungry for something new to read, so I plunged into the book; to say that I was overwhelmed by Lewis's wonderful tale would be an understatement. All I know is that, in spite of the fact that we were in the middle of final exams, I read the other six Narnian tales over the next day or two—I was hooked. And, thankfully, I did well enough on my exams to pass all of my courses in spite of my extra-curricular reading.

That was my introduction to Lewis. I was drawn to him through his imaginative books, but as I continued reading Lewis, I kept discovering new books by him on wide-ranging topics. It seemed Lewis had written books that scratched all my itches, and this was especially true with regard to literary studies. Having just become a Christian, I was looking forward to a course on John Milton that featured an extended study of *Paradise Lost*. I had heard that *Paradise Lost* was a distinctively Christian piece of literature, so I was primed for a rich literary experience, assuming that it would be informed by Milton's Christian perspective. I was not disappointed. Yet what most amazed me was that, once again, Lewis had been there before me. A required supplemental text in the course was Lewis's little masterpiece *A Preface to "Paradise Lost."* What a brilliant bit of literary scholarship! I still marvel at Lewis's insight into Milton's Satan; Lewis says that it is much easier for a writer to create a character much worse than himself, while very difficult to create a character who is far better. There is a depth of literary and spiritual insight in the passage that is hardly equaled anywhere else.

I think it was about at this same time that I first read *The Screwtape Letters*, the book of Lewis's that I reread most. I come back to this book so often because it so incisively describes the psychology of temptation from the hellish side. Screwtape is brilliantly drawn. He is no Underwood-deviled-ham devil. Instead, he writes with a stiletto; by means of his lucid, diabolical epistles he offers a disturbing insight into the nature of temptation. As a result, instead of glib, prepackaged, spiritual truisms, this book offers a sort of spiritual backhand; the slaps are painful and a bit unnerving. At the same time, Lewis's fascinating insights into the psychology of temptation are more nourishing than the devotional pabulum mass-produced by some Christian publishers. *The Screwtape Letters* is an antidevotional demanding we take serious stock of our spiritual lives.

It is tempting to wonder how Lewis will be viewed in another hundred years. Will he still be as popular in 2109 as he is in 2009? Which of his works will endure? How will his work influence the next several generations? Great questions, and not easy to answer. Almost certainly works like the Chronicles of Narnia and his Christian apologetics will endure much longer than his scholarly work. And Lewis's influence will never completely fade; he may be remembered by future generations as a composite of John Milton, John Bunyan, and Dr. Samuel Johnson. Lofty comparisons, but deservedly so.

All I know is that he has been a pivotal person in my literary, intellectual, and spiritual life. Each of us should find a writer we can read for the rest of our lives. It doesn't really matter whether the writer is well known to the rest of the world. What matters is that he or she *speaks* to us. For me that writer is C. S. Lewis; he combines literary excellence, hard-nosed thinking, and a winsome faith in Christ. It is no exaggeration to say he was the most articulate Christian writer of the twentieth century, especially in his appeal to readers across denominational lines. Although I never met him, through his books he became my greatest teacher and most influential mentor.

On the faculty of Montreat College since 1974, **Don W. King** is professor of English and serves as editor of the *Christian Scholar's Review*. His many articles have been published in *Books & Culture*, *The Canadian C. S. Lewis Journal*, *Christianity and Literature*, *The Bulletin of the New York C. S. Lewis Society*, *Mythlore*, *SEVEN: An Anglo-American Literary Review*, and others. King is also author of *C. S. Lewis, Poet: The Legacy of His Poetic Impulse* (Kent State University Press, 2008). He is currently researching and writing two manuscripts on the life, poetry, fiction, and nonfiction of C. S. Lewis's wife, Joy Davidman: *Out of My Bone: The Letters of Joy Davidman* and *Yet One More Spring: A Critical Study of the Works of Joy Davidman*.

38

A Commitment Based on Hard Evidence

John C. Lennox

When I arrived in Cambridge to study mathematics in 1962, a fellow student suggested to me that my faith in God was purely culturally dependent—merely a product of my Irish heritage and of no more significance beyond that. This presented me, a prospective scientist interested in the truth about the universe, with an immediate intellectual challenge.

But there was another of my fellow-countrymen at Cambridge, Professor C. S. Lewis, who had given careful thought to this very question. In his brilliant book *Mere Christianity* he asserted that the moral behavior of human beings from all cultures pointed toward the existence of a moral code that transcended culture. What is more, he showed that this is exactly what one would expect on the basis of the biblical account of the status of human life as created in the image of God.

For me Lewis has been and is a destroyer of popular myths that lie behind many of the objections made against my faith in God and Christ. For instance, Lewis showed that, far from involving an irrational leap in the dark, the Christian faith is a commitment based on hard evidence that is accessible to all. Not only that, but he also rapidly disposed of the false notion that science does not involve faith by observing that no science could be done without prior faith in the rational intelligibility of the universe. Furthermore, he pointed out that belief in the rational intelligibility of the universe makes perfect sense if the Christian worldview, with its central belief in a Creator, is true. On the other hand, he argued that belief in rationality itself is destroyed by the reductionist-atheist-materialist view that holds that the universe and life are nothing but the end product of unguided forces operating on matter.

Lewis's book *Miracles* helped me to see the flaws in David Hume's oft-cited arguments against miracles in general and the resurrection of Jesus Christ in particular. Against the prevalent notion that miracles "break the laws of nature," Lewis argued that the laws of nature are not causes but, rather, are our descriptions of what normally happens, so that the Creator, who is ultimately responsible for the regularities in the cosmos, is not a prisoner of those regularities. He is perfectly free to feed something new into the system. It is therefore absurd to suggest that science has shown that God could not encode himself into human life ("the Word became flesh" John 1:14 NKJV).

These books helped me to perceive the deep harmony between science and theology, a harmony that the advance of science in my lifetime has done nothing but confirm.

However, there is more to life than science. Lewis's book *The Problem of Pain* helped me to begin to come to grips with what is the hardest problem of all for a thinking Christian. Lewis did not offer simplistic answers, but with both intellectual fearlessness and remarkable emotional sensitivity he drew attention to the fact that the cross that stands at the very heart of the Christian message shows that God has not remained distant from human suffering. He has become part of it. The solutions to the problem of pain and to the problem of sin are related.

C. S. Lewis helped me to become an intellectually fulfilled Christian. I owe him a great debt.

John C. Lennox, M.A., Ph.D., D.Phil., D.Sc., is Reader in Mathematics at the University of Oxford and Fellow in Mathematics and Philosophy of Science at Green College. He is particularly interested in the interface between science, philosophy, and theology; he writes on science and religion, and he lectures widely. He is the author of *God's Undertaker: Has Science Buried God?* (Lion and Kregel, 2007) and recently represented the Christian worldview in a debate with Richard Dawkins. Dr. Lennox has also published widely in mathematics journals and has coauthored two mathematical monographs for Oxford University Press. He enjoys bird-watching and languages. He and his wife, Sally, have three children and four grandchildren.

39

Recovering Truth

LAWRENCE J. MACALA

In *The Everlasting Man*, G. K. Chesterton starts by saying, "There are two ways of getting home; and one of them is to stay there. The other is to walk round the whole world till we come back to the same place." I took the other way, the long road home. I was raised Catholic, but when I was about nineteen years old, I left the church.

I had no faith; I was lost and didn't even know it. Yet I set out on a road to find "Truth." I decided that it would have to be a truth of my own. I began by reading. I read whatever came across my path that I believed could lead me to the truth, whether it was Western or Eastern thought. The road would be long; it lasted ten years.

My intent was to create my own worldview from anything I found to my liking. My first stop was in coming to the realization that with regard to the question of God, I was now an agnostic. It took me some time to recognize the cowardice of such a position. One could not avoid the question of whether or not God exists. I decided that I had to answer that question. I went from the frying pan into the fire. I became an atheist. Little did I know how dark the road was becoming. I believed that the truth could still be known apart from God and that my personal discovery of the truth would satisfy my deepest need. I began to live by what Chesterton referred to in *The Everlasting Man* as "the circular argument by which everything begins and ends in the mind." I didn't know that at the end of that road there would be no hope, no peace, no joy, but only despair. I was living in the dungeon of my own mind.

My next leg of the journey was in believing that if there were truth, it would have to be discovered by science. Nothing else held the certainty of being true, and even if science did not arrive at any final truth, at least I could pursue it with the hope of finding it. Science had become my god. With this hope I began a career in science (which has lasted almost thirty years). In my very first job I worked daily with a doctor who was a Christian. The conversations were spirited. In my arrogance I considered that my scientific/atheistic worldview "won" every argument that we had. The dungeon walls were impenetrable.

A number of times, no doubt feeling frustrated, my colleague would simply say, "You should read C. S. Lewis's *Mere Christianity*; it will answer a lot of your questions." I thought to myself, *Why would a convinced atheist read anything about Christianity?* It was beyond me why an atheist would even buy a copy of *Mere Christianity*, but I did. Lewis divides his *Mere Christianity* into four books. The last three books are specifically Christian; after reading them, I thought they had some "nice" ideas and interesting "stuff," but it really meant nothing to me. It was book 1, which is not specifically Christian, that unsettled my thinking. Lewis argues in a profound way that there is a "Law of Human Nature" or "Moral Law" and that, whether we realize it or not, we all live by this law. More importantly, we all are breaking this law every day. What Lewis argues for is the reasonableness of theism. I didn't know it at the time, but Lewis's argument had made a small crack in the dungeon wall, and the faintest beam of light had entered in. I had come across an argument I could not answer. My atheism was now in doubt.

The next thing I knew I was reading a copy of the New Testament, which my Christian co-worker had given me. I began at the beginning. I read Matthew, Mark, and Luke. But it wasn't until I had read the Gospel of John and was just beginning the book of Acts that it happened: the dungeon flamed with light. It was as if a light switch had been flipped. What was once darkness immediately became light. In an instant I knew that it was all true. In fact, it was Truth. Jesus was indeed the Christ, the Son of the living God, God incarnate, the Savior of the world, and now my personal Savior. And even though I had only ever read a small fraction of the Old and New Testaments, in an instant I also knew that the Bible was absolutely true from beginning to end, every word. In that same instant the entire worldview that I had constructed over the last ten years came crashing down. I knew that all truth must now be God's truth. I had been set free from the dungeon of my mind. To quote the Charles Wesley hymn:

> Long my imprisoned spirit lay,
> Fast bound in sin and nature's night;
> Thine eye diffused a quickening ray;
> I woke, the dungeon flamed with light;
> My chains fell off, my heart was free,
> I rose, went forth, and followed thee.

I had made my own road for ten years. Lewis, by the grace of God, helped to show me my way back home. I am now free. Not only do I know the Truth, but also I know him who is the way, the truth, and the life; and it is his life that he wants all of us to live. So in response I rose, went forth, and followed Christ; and, as Lewis said, "Following Him is, of course, the essential point."

There is much value in reading Lewis as a skeptic, as an agnostic, or even as an atheist; but there is even greater value in reading him as a believer in Christ. G. K. Chesterton described the cure for "the circular argument by which everything begins and ends in the mind." He said, "Christianity does appeal to a solid truth outside itself; to something which is in that sense external as well as eternal." In *The Problem of Pain* Lewis refers to this same external world where we have three helps in recognizing the impact of God upon us: "the tradition of the Church, Holy Scripture, and the conversation of religious friends." Lewis is one of those friends. His works of fantasy, science fiction, apologetics, and literary criticism help us to see the truth of another world, which is very foreign to the modern world that surrounds us.

We are living in a time when "truth has stumbled in the street" (Isa. 59:14 NASB), and the Truth needs to be rediscovered and recovered if we are to truly live as God created us to live. We need, as Lewis said, to be reenchanted. He puts it this way in what I consider to be his best essay (and possibly his best work), "The Weight of Glory":

> Spells are used for breaking enchantments as well as for inducing them. And you and I have need of the strongest spell that can be found to wake us from the evil enchantment of worldliness which has been laid upon us for nearly a hundred years. Almost our whole education has been directed to silencing this shy, persistent, inner voice; almost all our modern philosophies have been devised to convince us that the good of man is to be found on this earth.

Indeed, we need to be reenchanted; reenchanted by the Truth and by him who is the Truth.

For the past twenty-five years **Lawrence J. Macala** has worked in biological research at the Yale University School of Medicine. A lifelong resident of Connecticut, he lives in Durham with his wife of thirty-two years, Diane. They have three grown children. He enjoys reading, walking, and conversation with friends. He and some of these friends created the Connecticut Christian Reading and Discussion Group, focusing on the works of C. S. Lewis and dedicated to reading and discussing Christian works of literature.

40

Screwtape and Steve

David Madio

The journey that brought me to C. S. Lewis was a long one. I was raised in a good home by loving parents. We were a churchgoing family that took our faith seriously. Every Sunday all of us not only attended worship services but also went to Sunday school classes. Both of my parents served on church boards and committees. Even on vacations we would always find a church to attend.

As I grew older, I sang in the choirs and was active in our junior high and senior high youth fellowships, holding leadership positions. I was quite serious about my faith. In our Baptist tradition, children at about the age of twelve attended baptism classes and were then baptized. I did all of this with great solemnity, but also excitement. It was the early 1970s, a period of great social activism, and baptism carried with it the right of full membership in the church, including being able to vote at all church meetings and being able to take communion. Baptism was as much a social rite of passage as it was a spiritual declaration.

Somehow in spite of many years in church, I never really understood the central message of the gospel. Christianity to me was a list of dos and don'ts. Good Christians followed those lists; bad Christians or non-Christians didn't. Even attending a Billy Graham evangelistic film with my youth group and going forward at the conclusion didn't remove the veil from my eyes.

When I went to college, my lifestyle quickly changed. I was exposed to and participated in many of the opportunities afforded to me at an elite, secular liberal arts college—some good, some not. I began to wrestle with the veracity of my faith. Free from my parents' supervision, I stopped attending church regularly. In short order, Sunday mornings became a time to sleep in, do laundry, and study. However, I had many discussions about religion with Steve, my roommate. I didn't know it at the time, but he had met and accepted Jesus as his Lord and Savior a few years earlier. At some point along the way, I concluded that one could be either intellectually honest or a Christian, but not both. I was torn by this, because actually I wanted to be both.

One of the great things about my college was that students could ask a professor to teach a tailor-made course, or tutorial. Toward the end of the fall semester of my junior year, a group of students, many of whom attended the evangelical student fellowship on campus, found a professor who was willing to examine some of C. S. Lewis's works. Steve invited me to register for the class.

I borrowed *The Screwtape Letters* from the public library during the Christmas holiday to see if the course would interest me. In it Lewis allows his readers to follow the imagined correspondence of Screwtape to his nephew, Wormwood. As a senior demon, Screwtape is seeking to instruct Wormwood in how to control, deceive, and manipulate the human "patient" assigned to him. Before I had finished the first letter, I was hooked.

As I continued to read, the book moved from thought-provoking fiction to reality. I was stunned! I had entertained just these types of thoughts on numerous occasions. So it was settled; I would take the course.

The first book assigned in the course was *Surprised by Joy: The Shape of My Early Life*. In it Lewis describes how he "passed from Atheism to Christianity." As I read, I began to see from the arguments he presented that Christianity was not an unreasonable faith. A brilliant scholar who taught at both Oxford and Cambridge, Lewis showed me that I did not need to choose between intellectual honesty and Christianity. It actually seemed that if one were intellectually honest, one would in fact be drawn to Christianity.

As the course continued, we read many other works by Lewis—*The Four Loves*, *The Problem of Pain*, *A Grief Observed*, *The Great Divorce*, and the Chronicles of Narnia. To prepare for my final paper, I read the often-overlooked *Till We Have Faces*, a wonderful retelling of an ancient myth from a Christian perspective. I was a physics major used to reading only about thirty pages per week for a course, so I was in over my head in this humanities seminar. Although I often was behind in my reading, I did listen carefully to our discussions. Much to my surprise, it was the evangelical students, the ones who took the Bible texts seriously, whose arguments seemed the most reasonable.

Before the course had ended, I had become convinced that Christianity was true. My time at college had been a gradual drift away from upright behavior, however. Nothing awful, but things I knew were displeasing to God, things to which I had grown attached. So I put off making a decision until a chance encounter with Steve at the beach during the summer moved him to write me a note. When I received his note, I decided I would do what he suggested but then promptly forgot about it.

A few weeks later as I was straightening my desk, I came across the note. I decided to follow Steve's advice to "give Jesus a try for a day." This was not a typical evangelistic message, nor was my response a typical sinner's prayer. I simply got up one morning and told God that I would try to do what he wanted for that day. I was quite sincere, but before long, the busyness of work pushed my promise to God far from my mind.

A couple of weeks later I recognized that I was in a pretty good mood. In fact, I noted, I had been in a good mood the previous day as well. Suddenly it dawned on me—it had been two weeks since I had prayed that prayer. Now I knew that it was all true, that Jesus was alive, that my sins could be forgiven—I had been born anew! Like Lewis, I had been surprised by joy! My whole life changed. Now I couldn't wait to get home from work to read the Bible. I was like a dry sponge soaking up the water of the Word; for the first time it really made sense to me. I couldn't help but tell people about the greatest news in the world.

In the years since, I have had time to reread some of Lewis's works at a more leisurely pace. As I did, *The Silver Chair* found a special place in my heart. It is the story of a Narnian prince held captive through deception by an evil queen. The lion Aslan, King of Narnia, summons Jill and Eustace to Narnia to rescue the prince. With great skill, Lewis highlights the Christian's walk in this book. Almost from the beginning, Aslan's plan seems to get disrupted repeatedly, first by bickering between Jill and Eustace. Then Jill fails to continue to meditate on the Five Signs that Aslan has told her to watch for, and she and Eustace often fail to recognize the signs because they don't appear as they'd imagined. Puddleglum, whose name captures his general outlook, is added to their rescue party. After their rescue proves successful, Puddleglum is still, well . . . Puddleglum. But Jill has grown to see that despite his doleful manner and fearfulness, he really was "as brave as—as a lion."

Lewis wonderfully intertwines two deep themes in *The Silver Chair*: things and people often don't appear as we expect, yet God is sovereign. As I continue this Christian journey, those lessons become increasingly important to me. I find myself continually thankful that "if we are faithless, [God] remains faithful—for he cannot deny himself" (2 Tim. 2:13 ESV).

David Madio holds a Ph.D. in physics from the University of Pittsburgh, specializing in nuclear magnet resonance (NMR), particularly imaging (MRI). He currently works for a worldwide oil-field services company, analyzing data acquired in oil-well boreholes and developing new ways to extract even more data from them. He and his wife, Sally, live in Sugar Land, Texas.

41

Starving for Heavenly Food

WAYNE MARTINDALE

I begin with a confession. I have not always wanted to go to heaven. I can see now that many myths had unconsciously crowded into my mind: fuzzy logic conspired with pictures of stuffy mansion houses and ghosts walking on golden (therefore barren and cold) streets. Perhaps my biggest fear, until some time after my undergraduate years, was that heaven would be boring.

I knew I should want to go to heaven but I didn't. I would have said that I want to go to heaven when I die, but mainly, I just didn't want to go to hell. My problem was a badly warped theology and a thoroughly starved imagination. I knew that in heaven we would worship God forever. But the only model I had for worship was church, and frankly, I wasn't in love with church enough to want it to go on through ages of ages, world without end. My mental image was of Reverend Cant droning on forever and ever.

Somewhere in the back of my mind, quite unconsciously, heaven was an extended, boring church service like those I had not yet learned to appreciate on earth—with this exception: you never got to go home to the roast beef dinner. What a way to anticipate my eternal destiny. But then I read C. S. Lewis's *The Great Divorce*. It awakened in me an appetite for something better than roast beef. It aroused a longing to inherit what I was created for: that which would fulfill my utmost longings and engender new longings and fulfill those, too. After reading *The Great Divorce*, for the first time in my life I felt heaven to be both utterly real and utterly desirable. It was a magnificent gift. Small wonder, then, that *The Great Divorce* has always been one of my favorite books, because when I read it, it awakened me to my spiritual anorexia. I was starving for heavenly food and didn't even know I was hungry.

On the final page of *The Last Battle* we hear these wonderful words: "For them it was only the beginning of the real story. All their life in this world and all their adventures in Narnia had only been the cover and the title page: now at last they were beginning Chapter One of the Great Story which no one on earth has read: which goes on forever: in which every chapter is better than the one before."

This account is taken from Martindale's introduction to *Beyond the Shadowlands: C. S. Lewis on Heaven and Hell*, and is reprinted with permission from the publisher, Crossway Books, a division of Good News Publishers, Wheaton, IL 60187, www.crossway.com.

Wayne Martindale, an English professor at Wheaton College since 1981, was introduced to C. S. Lewis by a college professor when he was twenty. He had no idea that he would later read all the works of Lewis and would coedit, along with Jerry Root, *The Quotable Lewis*. Martindale states unashamedly, "C. S. Lewis was my spiritual mentor."

42

C. S. Lewis's Impact on My Faith

Thomas S. Monaghan

I've never read anything that hit me as hard as "The Great Sin" by C. S. Lewis. It's a short chapter from one of his books [*Mere Christianity*], but after I read it, I stayed up most of the night reviewing my life. As I did, I realized that a lot of the things about me that I thought were good—being competitive, driving for success, always trying harder than anybody else—weren't necessarily that good after all.

I had worked hard at my business, sacrificing and doing without so that I could have more later. I had to have the best, to be the best, and I asked myself why. Was it largely because I wanted to be better than others?

Lewis writes, "We say that people are proud of being rich, or clever, or good-looking, but they are not. They are proud of being richer, or cleverer, or better looking than others. It is the comparison that makes you proud: the pleasure of being above the rest." That was a dose of reality for me. What I'd thought of as a virtue—the drive to be better and have more than others—turned out to be a vice. It wasn't *what* I was doing that was bad, Lewis said, but *why* I was doing it.

What a shock! I immediately thought of the one thing I was obsessed with, the project that consumed my time and enthusiasm: my dream house. As a frustrated architect, I'd been planning it for years. I spent hours dreaming about it, reading about it, looking at designs, thinking up new features that would make it unique. It had become my passion. But when I realized what was really driving me—the desire to have something no one else had—I knew what had to be done, and my wife Margie had no objection. Even though the foundation was already in and the construction was one-third completed, we stopped work on it the next morning.

I was amazed to discover that this single decision gave me an immediate sense of freedom. I found myself more content and more at peace. I was able to refocus my time on activities that reflect ultimate concerns and goals. Chuck Colson, the former White House special counsel, says that it was this very chapter that changed the course of his life. It did the same for me.

The above reflections were written by Mr. Monaghan in 1991, soon after reading the chapter entitled "The Great Sin" in *Mere Christianity*. It is used with permission of the Ave Maria Foundation.

Although best known as the founder of Domino's Pizza and former owner of the Detroit Tigers baseball franchise, **Thomas S. Monaghan** is currently devoting his attention full-time to nonprofit endeavors specifically focused on underwriting Catholic higher education. This support primarily flows through the Ave Maria Foundation, which he founded in 1983. He is also founder and chancellor of Ave Maria University, located in the new town of Ave Maria, Florida. He and his wife, Marjorie, have four daughters and eight grandchildren. (The house mentioned above remains unfinished.)

43

Like a Very Good Rainstorm

Earl F. Palmer

C. S. Lewis the writer broke in upon my life like a very good rainstorm while I was an undergraduate at the University of California, Berkeley. My first C. S. Lewis book was *The Screwtape Letters*, and this small book has remained one of the most influential books upon my life.

Lewis has a way of asking questions that I want to ask and a way of thinking up stories and analysis to go with the questions that always help me to see more clearly the most important things to see. He is a storyteller who loves stories of the fantastic. I owe him a great debt in helping me grasp the greatest of all stories—the one that is both wonderfully fantastic and yet true.

Lewis never wasted a word, and so I owe him that love of economy of language, too. There is an integrity in his spareness that works on me to keep my words honest.

Finally, I appreciate all those little pieces of the puzzle that have come together to help me understand the man. He was reserved, interior, honest, rumpled, witty, thoughtful, strong-willed, nonstylish in appearance, yet with a face that was arresting and generous. I have wondered if the lad Shasta in *The Horse and His Boy* is not the self-portrait of C. S. Lewis after all.

This account first appeared in *Count Your Blessings* by Victor Bogard (privately published) and is reprinted with permission.

Earl F. Palmer is senior pastor of Seattle's University Presbyterian Church. He often speaks about the writings of Lewis to his congregation of 4,500 members and to national and international audiences. He is also a frequent presenter at Seattle Pacific University's C. S. Lewis Institute.

44

The Joy of Being Surprised by C. S. Lewis

Joseph Pearce

I first stumbled across C. S. Lewis while fumbling around in a fog of ignorance. As an angry young man, filled to the brim with bitterness, I was groping for fragments of light amid figments of darkness. The light had first shone forth from the pages of a book by G. K. Chesterton, *The Well and the Shallows*, in which the intellectually indefatigable GKC had vanquished many of the idols of my prejudice. I began to perceive, dimly at first, that the philosophy and theology of Christendom were the well of truth from which European civilization had sprung whereas the ideas of modernity were mere shallows by comparison.

I developed a seemingly insatiable appetite for Chesterton, scouring through secondhand bookshops for his works. It was on one of these book-trawling expeditions that my eyes settled on a book called *Surprised by Joy* by someone called C. S. Lewis. I had heard of C. S. Lewis, possibly as the author of *The Lion, the Witch and the Wardrobe* (a book I'd never read), but I knew nothing about him. Perhaps I had read somewhere that he was a Christian writer. Perhaps not. I'm not sure. The shadow of the years has descended upon the surface of my memory. Either way, something prompted me to take the book from the shelf. Thumbing through the pages, I looked for references to Chesterton and, sure enough, soon stumbled across his name in Chapter XII. My interest aroused, I quickly devoured those pages. As my eyes read Lewis's word, my heart leapt, surprised by the joy of discovering a kindred spirit. "It was here that I first read a volume of Chesterton's essays," Lewis wrote. "I had never heard of him and had no idea of what he stood for; nor can I quite understand why he made such an immediate conquest of me." Yes! This was exactly how I felt when I had first read him. It was uncanny that someone in a field hospital in France during the First World War, more than sixty years earlier, could have felt exactly the same way that I had upon discovering Chesterton. I continued reading.

"It might have been expected that my pessimism, my atheism, and my hatred of sentiment would have made him to me the least congenial of authors. It would almost seem that Providence, or some 'second cause' of a very obscure kind, quite over-rules our previous tastes when It decides to bring two minds together." Exactly! I couldn't have put it better myself. "Liking an author may be as involuntary and improbable as falling in love." Yes again! How did this man Lewis do it? He knew exactly how I felt about Chesterton. He knew it because he felt it, too—in exactly the same way.

Lewis waxed lyrical about Chesterton for a further page or so, my heart continually leaping in joyful ascent at his words, before he finally concluded with the following doom-laden words: "In reading Chesterton . . . I did not know what I was letting myself in for. A young man who wishes to remain a sound Atheist cannot be too careful of his reading. There are traps everywhere. . . . God is, if I may say it, very unscrupulous."

After reading these words, I couldn't say that I hadn't been warned. Lewis was cautioning me that, in reading Chesterton, I was walking a dangerous path. Who knew where it might lead? The warning went unheeded. Not only did I not desist from reading Chesterton, but I now added C. S. Lewis as a literary mentor. From now on, when trawling through the treasures in secondhand bookshops, I would be searching for titles by Lewis as well as those by Chesterton.

In reading Lewis's *Mere Christianity*, as in reading Chesterton's *Orthodoxy*, I learned that the Christian creed provided the very credentials for truth itself. In reading Lewis's *The Problem of Pain*, as in reading Chesterton's *The Man Who Was Thursday*, I began to perceive the sense to be found in suffering; and in reading *A Grief Observed* I saw the abstract arguments about suffering become incarnate in Lewis's own pain at losing his wife. In Narnia, as in Chesterton's *Manalive* and his Father Brown stories, I discovered the wonder of remaining childlike and the wisdom that springs from this wonder-filled innocence. And, of course, in Lewis, as in Chesterton, there was so much more to discover. Finally, through their guidance, like John in *The Pilgrim's Regress*, I would lay myself at the feet of Mother Kirk. In reading the works of Lewis and Chesterton, and in the enjoyment of their company, I had crossed the threshold of hope and had entered Aslan's country.

Joseph Pearce is a writer-in-residence and associate professor of literature at Ave Maria University in Naples, Florida. He is the author of many books, including *Lewis and the Catholic Church* and *Wisdom and Innocence: A Life of G. K. Chesterton*, and he is coeditor of the *Saint Austin Review*, a journal of Christian culture (www.staustinreview.com).

45

He Rings True

Pierce Pettis

I was introduced to C. S. Lewis by a philosophy professor who happened to be Roman Catholic. He had us read *The Abolition of Man* when I was about nineteen or twenty years old and an undergraduate at Florida State University. I was particularly struck by the chapter "Men without Chests." I can't remember if I was a Christian or even a theist yet, but that little book made a big impression on me. Afterwards I thought, *Gee, I should read more of this guy*, and eventually I did: *Mere Christianity*, *The Screwtape Letters*, *The Problem of Pain*, *Till We Have Faces*, *A Grief Observed*, and more.

I've always been impressed by Lewis's intellectual honesty. I love the way he can be profound in such simple, concise language. He says precisely what he means, using examples that make sense and often with a great deal of wit.

I can see how some would not agree with Lewis, but it's hard to imagine anyone who would not like and respect him. Lewis has challenged me, personally, to say what I mean and mean what I say. Also, he challenges me to make no assumptions and to be prepared to defend what I say with facts, not opinions.

Lewis also motivated me to read some of the people who inspired him—particularly G. K. Chesterton and George MacDonald, as well as the other Inklings. And, as a side note, I find it interesting that this Irish Protestant was converted to the faith by an English Roman Catholic (Tolkien). Lewis also claims that his two biggest influences, theologically, were a Roman Catholic apologist and a Presbyterian minister—evidence that God suffers no sectarians.

Lewis strikes me as a man who lived his faith in a way that was practical and humble. He showed me that Christian faith is not the end of intellectual curiosity but the beginning ("the fear of the Lord is the beginning of wisdom," Prov. 9:10 KJV). But more importantly, I see in his personal life a genuine Christlike spirit in the way he took pains to answer personally the hundreds and hundreds of letters he received; his relationship with Joy Davidman and her sons; his devotion to his brother; and his companionship with J. R. R. Tolkien, Charles Williams, Dorothy L. Sayers, Owen Barfield, Hugo Dyson, and so many others.

My experience with Lewis is that he rings true with me, personally. Something in me resounds when, for example, he boldly proclaims that Christ cannot be a mere prophet (as polite society would like to portray him), but he must be taken as either a madman imposter or the Messiah—the Son of God he claims to be. There are very few Christian writers who have this effect on me.

A native Alabaman, **Pierce Pettis** began his musical career in 1979 when Joan Baez covered one of his songs, "Song at the End of the Movie," on her album *Honest Lullaby*. Since then he has performed in forty-eight states, Canada, and Europe and has released several albums. In 1999 Pettis received the Country Music Award from ASCAP for "You Move Me," co-written with Gordon Kennedy and recorded by Garth Brooks on his album *Sevens*.

46

I Look to Lewis All the Time

Anne Rice Encounters C. S. Lewis

Anne Rice with Mary Anne Phemister

"Why is Anne Rice, once the literary queen of darkness, now writing about Christ, the light of the world?" asks Cindy Crosby in her article "Interview with a Penitent" (*Christianity Today*, December 2005). A self-described atheist prior to 1998, Rice began to read obsessively about the Jews, Christianity, and the Bible. "The Lord came looking for me," she told Crosby. "Everywhere I turned, I found images of the Lord and his love." As she conducted research for her novel *Christ the Lord: Out of Egypt*, Rice was particularly impressed by N. T. Wright's book *The Resurrection of the Son of God*. "Christianity achieved what it did," she affirms, "because Jesus rose from the dead." Later she claimed, "Writing *Christ the Lord* means more to me than anything I've ever done."

"Christians have been arguing with each other for 2,000 years," Rice continues in the interview with Crosby. To Christians who disagree with her views, she states, "What I hope for is that we can love one another, no matter how much we disagree. . . . If we love, we can overcome much of what divides us as a people." Attesting to her new-found faith, she continues, "I've had wonderful experiences as a writer. I've stepped out of limos in New York City to crowds wanting autographs and embracing me. There are no words for that. But this is the biggest adventure of my life. Thrilling beyond everything."

In an email message to the editor of this volume, Anne Rice describes her encounter with C. S. Lewis:

> I didn't really read Lewis until I was on a book tour for my novel *Christ the Lord*. I read his *Mere Christianity* and thought it a brilliant and affirming book. It helped me to clarify for myself and for others what had happened to me in my return to the church. I look to Lewis all the time for inspiration. Earlier, the film *Shadowlands* had influenced me with its picture of Lewis's scholarly life in England and his love for his new bride. What really moved me in Lewis's books was the simple, understandable eloquence of his explanations of what Christianity was about; he went to the heart of it; I found it bold and clear. That's what I search for, books that can make the complex and the seemingly irreconcilable very simple and clear. Lewis helps one to defend the faith, to explain the faith . . . and to embrace the faith.

Anne Rice, best known for her Vampire Chronicles and horror/fantasy stories, declared in the *Christianity Today* interview that she will never again write another vampire novel, saying, "I would never go back, not even if they say, 'You will be financially ruined; you've got to write another Vampire book.' I would say no. I have no choice. I would be a fool for all eternity to turn my back on God like that." Widowed after forty-one years of marriage to Stan Rice, a high school classmate, Anne Rice now lives in Rancho Mirage, California, not far from her novelist son, Christopher. Her book *Christ the Lord: The Road to Cana* was published in March 2008.

47

A Vocabulary for My Soul

JERRY ROOT

I grew up surrounded by family members who were readers, but not me. I was more interested in playing with a football or pole-vaulting than picking up a book. I had no academic interest or inclination. Nevertheless, it was sports that got me into college, and interest in staying eligible kept me in college. During my freshman year my older brother, Chester, and his roommate, Mark, took me to a meeting where I heard the gospel clearly presented for the first time. I became a Christian. That year I read the Bible through from cover to cover, a habit that I've sought to continue most years ever since. My mind woke up. I started reading Christian literature and would see C. S. Lewis's name pop up from time to time, but I knew nothing about him.

During spring break of my junior year, my roommate, Chris, and I went to San Francisco to visit my sister and her family. Kathy was teaching school at the time, and she was reading *The Lion, the Witch and the Wardrobe* to her students. Over dinner she told us the plot of the book. I was deeply moved by the story. The next day Chris and I were riding our bikes throughout the city, and we happened on a bookstore in the Cannery near Fisherman's Wharf. There was a huge display of boxed sets of the Narnian Chronicles, so I bought my first Lewis books. That was in 1970.

Over the next several weeks I read all the books in the series and wanted desperately to bury my face in Aslan's mane. I also wanted more books by this guy named Lewis. I learned that he had written an autobiography, so I read *Surprised by Joy* next. This was the book that really hooked me on Lewis. As he described his pilgrimage to faith and the fact that he was driven in a quest to find the object of the deep longings that had haunted him since childhood, I could identify. In fact, I knew the longings he wrote about but had never heard anyone else speak of them or read anyone who wrote about them. Lewis gave me a vocabulary for my soul. I was hungry for anything by Lewis I could get my hands on, and I read voraciously. I even started reading the books he referred to in his writings. One philosophy professor, Michael Praetorius, who taught at Whittier College, where I attended, required Lewis for several of his courses. I took every class he offered and couldn't believe that I could get college credit for reading Lewis. My whole world started opening up to me.

When I was about ready to graduate, an acquaintance told me that he didn't think anyone received an education in college. I wondered why I had paid so much in tuition if that was the case. Then my friend wisely noted that college only allows one to lay the foundation for an education, and "commencement" means that one can begin one's education by building on that foundation. He then advised me that I should pick an author who would take me places and make a lifelong study of that author. I was reading many authors by this time. All had a depth to them, but none had the breadth of Lewis. All were serious about their subject matter, but none were as clear as Lewis. Each had insight, but none were as imaginative and delightful to read as Lewis. So the decision was easy; I picked Lewis as my life's author. I doubt that I could have done better. I began reading not only Lewis but dozens of the authors to whom he refers, starting with the classics and moving through medieval literature and on to the late nineteenth century and then on to Lewis's contemporaries in the twentieth century. Reading Lewis was a liberal arts education!

I've found that no true reader of Lewis will ever get stuck in a Lewis rut, nor will true readers of Lewis become overly fascinated with Lewis—he won't allow it. He is always deflecting attention away from himself and onto some item glorious in its own right and also infused with the presence of God. I've grown to appreciate what

Lewis once observed: every bush is a burning bush, and the world is crowded with God; he walks everywhere incognito. It remains for us to awaken to him and, even more, to remain awake.

Perhaps the most significant thing Lewis has done for me is to encourage development of my own Christian faith. He once wrote to an eleven-year-old girl, three weeks before he died, "If you continue to love Jesus, nothing much can go wrong with you, and I hope you may always do so." It is advice like this that helps me to put first things first, as he wisely advised. Furthermore, Lewis has expanded my faith and also validated my doubts; there will always be much we do not know or understand. He has helped me to understand the love of God in such a way that I could explore any question with a childlike confidence in the love of God and a freedom from fear. If the answers aren't forthcoming in days of ambiguity, Lewis encourages me to trust and love the One who holds the answers till they come. I've learned through him that if some of the gravest difficulties have produced good, given time, then I have good reason to suspect that, given eternity, all that's bad will be set right. Lewis's whole life was a testimony to this, and my own faith has grown through reading him.

Jerry Root pastored churches for over twenty-three years before he wrote his Ph.D. dissertation, *C. S. Lewis and a Problem of Evil: An Investigation of a Pervasive Theme* (Oxford: Open University). Besides editing (with Wayne Martindale) *The Quotable C. S. Lewis*, he has authored numerous articles and chapters in other books and frequently lectures on Lewis around the world. Professor Root managed to play American football until he was forty-four—without injury—and has coached and played American football in Oxford, England. He never misses a Wheaton College home game if he is in town. He lives in Wheaton with his wife, Claudia. They have four grown children.

48

Caught by Surprise

STEPHEN SAVAGE

Raised in a missionary family and educated in Christian schools, Stephen Savage had thrown it all over by midlife. "I had become a complete unbeliever," he wrote in a book about his father, a "rough-as-a-cob, old foot-stomping Baptist," who was also a musician, song-writer, radio personality, and preacher. Stephen wished that he could be a zealous Christian, if for no other reason than to please his father, but doubts about the faith continued to plague him. He says, "After years of trying to make sense out of it, I felt relieved to quit the effort." In his second marriage Stephen inherited two stepchildren, and he felt responsible for providing spiritual leadership for his wife's children.

I bought the Chronicles of Narnia by C. S. Lewis and began to read a couple of chapters per night to the children. They were spellbound by the hair-raising adventures of the marvelous creatures inhabiting that magic land. As the kids listened in fascination, they were sometimes puzzled when my voice choked and I was unable to keep reading. "Go on," they urged. I would clear my throat and continue.

To the children, the stories were sheer adventure. To me, they were a whole new way of looking at the Christian faith. I was jolted by the magic of Narnia. Aslan the Lion (a symbol of Christ) was compelling and caught me by surprise. I had answered every argument advanced in Christian apologetics, but suddenly my mind was bombarded from another angle. This was no mere fairy tale. Aslan, the great and majestic lion, attracted to his side the good people of the land of Narnia: the honest human girl, Lucy; the chivalrous and courageous mouse, Reepicheep; the majestic unicorn, Jewel; the steadfast fawn, Mr. Tumnus; the practical and good-hearted souls, Mr. and Mrs. Beaver; and many other fascinating and varied personalities, all bound together by qualities of decency, loyalty, courage, truthfulness, compassion, and humility. On the other side were the rascals, the followers of Jadis, the White Witch. One of them was Edmund, Lucy's brother, who was drawn under the witch's spell by his craving for Turkish Delight. Other followers of the witch were the wolves and some of the dwarves.

Throughout the seven books, the conflict between good and evil was portrayed vividly, both in day-to-day relationships among Narnia's creatures, as well as in the final battle that raged between the forces of light and darkness. In a way I had never seen before, I now saw the various faces of evil. And after years of feeling dull toward all spiritual talk, I found myself charmed with the supernatural. I was touched in a very particular way by the Great Lion, Aslan himself. I was impressed with the boundless, leaping joy he conferred on his country and the dread he elicited in those who feared and loathed him. Aslan voluntarily sacrificed his life to win back the betrayer, Edmund.

Fascinated, I went to several bookstores until I had bought every book Lewis had ever written—and devoured them all. His science fiction trilogy gave me yet another way of looking at the faith—in bright colors, vast spaces, and fantastic descriptions about the struggle between good and evil on other planets. It helped me feel the reality of the spiritual warfare here on earth.

A moment of drama came as I read *The Great Divorce* and suddenly found the idea of hell not altogether outrageous, for Lewis depicted it as a place people *chose to go*. I had viewed it as the vendetta of an angry God, who flung people into the cauldron, willy-nilly, simply because they hadn't quite figured out the story during their short journey on earth.

The doctrine of hell had been one unpalatable point of theology for me. The idea made it difficult for me to buy the Christian story. Now I had an alternative way to think about it. Lewis drew a picture of hell as a place of ever-increasing distance from God—because its inhabitants *preferred* it that way. They *always* had a choice to go back to heaven, but as time went on, they became more set in their ways and less likely to have any desire to return. Although Lewis did not set this forth as an actual doctrine of hell and advised his readers that his book was nothing more than a fantasy, it still gave me a way of dealing with the once-impossible topic.

In *The Great Divorce* each person was given many opportunities to choose. The ultimate choice was simple: "My will or thine." Those who preferred their own way of self-seeking aggrandizement were given precisely what they wanted. Those who said, "Thy will" were ushered into an eternity of delirious joy as they joined the throngs in heaven who chose to bow before their master and say, "Not my will, but thine."

One night I awoke at 2 a.m. much to my great discomfiture. I found myself praying that very prayer: "Not my will, but thine." Immediately I said to myself, *Hey, take it easy, Steve; don't get sucked in. This will fade away in a few days.* I was deeply suspicious of any emotional conversion experience, and I wanted to avoid any silliness.

Over the days and weeks ahead, however, the conviction stuck, and I found myself praying quite calmly and quite often as I went through each day, "Not my will, but thine." I became at ease with the prayer and even got a little emotional at times.

I wanted to tell Dad about all this, but hesitated, not wanting to get him too excited. I wasn't sure how long this would last, and I didn't want to arouse his expectations. For several months I kept it to myself and to Barrie, and continued to read Lewis's books. Then finally I visited Mom and Dad in Muskegon and described the events of the past few months. As my story unfolded, Dad became increasingly ecstatic. Finally, he could contain himself no longer. "Praise God!" he shouted. "My son has come back home!" I told him, "Dad, all these years I've wandered in the spiritual wilderness, and you never wavered in your love for me. I've seen a lot of parents reject their kids when they had problems with the faith, but you have stood by me all these years."

This account is taken from Stephen E. Savage's book *Rejoicing in Christ: The Biography of Robert Carlton Savage* and is used with permission of the author.

Stephen Savage is a real estate appraiser and pilot who lives with his wife, Barrie, in Atlanta, Georgia.

49

A Special Instrument of Grace

Nicholas Seward

I've always been a very patriotic Englishman, perhaps because of—rather than despite—the fact that I was born and brought up abroad. My parents were both teachers. My father was a physical education teacher and was quite idealistic; I would describe him as a child of the 1960s. He wanted to travel and to make a difference to children who would really appreciate and value their education (not often regarded as a hallmark of teaching in the state system in England!). That was how I ended up being born in Zambia and growing up in Papua New Guinea from when I was about seven years old. For some reason we ended up being posted in a mission station in the "back of beyond" in the Southern Highlands. I'm still not quite clear how my devoutly irreligious parents ended up there, but there it is. My mother was quite agnostic at the time (she has come back to her faith in recent years), and my father was quite vocally atheistic. He regarded religion as a pack of fairy tales, and our experience in the village of Dauli jaundiced his views further.

My parents were quite fair-minded with us as children—we were told that we would have to make up our own minds about religion, although it was clear where Dad stood, at least. I've always had faith in

God—I can't remember a time when I didn't—and I simply disagreed with Dad, not in any rebellious way, just that I had a sense of God's presence as a child. However, I do have a grandmother who is a stout old woman of faith. I have distant memories of her taking me to carol services in the interim between Zambia and Papua New Guinea. Ever since then I've loved English carols and their sense of the good news that *is* good news. I've never understood those who don't "get" the message. It was always as clear as a bell to me.

In Papua New Guinea my younger sister and I were sent to a boarding school run by European missionaries in the Southern Highlands. On at least two occasions my parents were admonished by the principal of this conservative school—first, for my playing tennis on the Sabbath, and second, because I was found to possess a book on dinosaurs—which they regarded as false history. Whatever the rights and wrongs of each situation, and however much my own memories are clouded or distorted by my parents' versions of events, the overall impression was not of welcoming Christian love. At the mission school we were constantly told that our parents were going to burn in hell. As a little boy who believed in Jesus, I felt great agonies upon hearing this. In my prayers I imagined being at the gates of heaven and facing the prospect of having to go in without my father.

Into the midst of all this fell the Narnia books, which I discovered in the school library. Above all else they awakened in me that ineffable yearning which C. S. Lewis calls *Sehnsucht*. It was perfectly clear to me what they were all about. I had already read parts of the Bible as a seven- or eight-year-old boy (often when I was in trouble!), and imprinted on my soul at that young age were words like, "Ask, and it shall be given you; seek, and ye shall find; knock, and it shall be opened unto you" (Matt. 7:7 KJV).

It is hard to put into words all that the Narnia books meant and still mean to me. One thing I remember vividly was rereading them again at about age thirteen. My father was conducting research for a master's degree in sport in remote Papua New Guinea villages and communities. His studies involved traveling by light aircraft into tiny jungle airstrips, and I tagged along for the ride. At one point we were spending some time at an old mission station on the mosquito-infested south coast. While Dad was out doing his work, I lay about in the shade, escaping the tropical heat and relieving the boredom by reading. I was astonished on reading the whole seven Narnia books again to feel that so much was *missing*. My imagination as a little boy had taken Lewis's words and built a vast and fantastical image of Narnia—its magic and glory, its kings and queens, and all the great tapestry of its history. I suppose what had really happened was that I had had a taste of that romantic experience that Lewis describes so well—a bright trail of "spilled glory," which, if faithfully followed, will bring you back to its divine source.

If I have a favorite of the series, it's *The Silver Chair*. As a boy I longed more than anything else in the world to be a Narnian, living an "ordinary" Narnian life. Above all, I loved the passages with Aslan but also the scenes describing the mixture of homeliness and magic of my "true country." The breakfast scene in *The Horse and His Boy* springs to mind, as does the winter dance and its aftermath (proper sausages!), when Jill emerges from the Underworld. The other books deal with what Lewis might have called the "great ganglions" of Narnian history, but *The Silver Chair* is a story about a relatively unremarkable period of history, involving ordinary Narnians in the business of trying to be faithful to Aslan. On top of that, I felt a mysterious symbolism and power behind the image of the eponymous Chair, much as I had in the breaking of the Stone Table earlier on in the series. I still haven't quite worked out what I think Lewis meant by it, but it exerted a numinous fascination over me then and since has felt full of mythopoeic power in my own struggle with sin.

I was in love with Aslan. I knew who he represented, and I knew, deep down, that the Narnia stories weren't really true in the way that the Bible was true. I wanted to be a Christian, and I made several moves towards trying to get more involved. I came back to England to go to school when I was twelve, traveling back to Papua New Guinea in the summers (including the one spent rereading the books). I joined my church youth group and went to a Billy Graham crusade with them. I went forward at the altar call, although I felt at the time as though I was making a *deeper* rather than a *first* commitment to Jesus. I have never been able to pinpoint a time when I was "born again," a source of considerable spiritual angst to me. I can look to important turning points, but I can also look back at episodes of wandering in the wilderness of sin, failing in my Christian witness (sometimes grievously), and periods of doubt and struggle with my faith.

I can't quite remember how I got hold of a copy of *Mere Christianity*, but it had a similar effect as the Narnia books. I was seventeen. I suppose I had been harboring a nagging suspicion that my faith would not stand up to intellectual scrutiny. Lewis's book made extraordinary sense. I remember thinking that everyone in the world ought to read it, and then it would be perfectly simple—everyone would become Christians, because it was impossible to argue with his defense of the faith! I felt myself convicted more powerfully of the reality of my sinfulness, particularly pride.

Not long after this I went to London to study engineering—a subject that didn't interest me much—but what kept me going were the books by C. S. Lewis. I devoured everything he had written. My great treat to myself was to buy a new book of essays or writings each fortnight. Everything he said made perfect sense to me. Not only his arguments, which were formidable enough, but I also sensed humility, vision, and honesty in every word. Lewis's imaginative writings like *The Great Divorce* or *The Screwtape Letters* seemed to me to be devastatingly accurate and true, in the deepest sense of the word. Every time I read anything he wrote, I felt freshly impelled to pursue holiness.

Holiness, I am afraid, escaped me, and exactly halfway through my course of study, the whole sorry edifice of my life came crashing down with the ending of the relationship I had been involved in. I thought any number of self-indulgent and destructive thoughts that evening, but in the midst of all the vain ruins of my pride, there seemed to be a still, small voice saying that Jesus still loved me. If ever there was a turning point in my Christian life, it was then. I realized that it was Jesus or nothing for me now.

A few years later, via a circuitous route, I found myself training for the ordained ministry, which included writing a master's thesis on Lewis's works entitled "A Fairy-Tale for Grown-Ups: Christian Orthodoxy in the Theology of C. S. Lewis." I now touched on the beginnings of a life's work, or at least a life's meditation, as I encountered for the first time some of the sources of Lewis's ideas and outlook—Rudolf Otto, St. Thomas Aquinas, Plato, and Baron von Hugel, to name a few.

After a curacy in the Diocese of Canterbury, where I met and married a lovely woman who shared my faith and admiration for Lewis and his friends (I'm also a great fan of Tolkien), providence brought me to Magdalen College School in Oxford as chaplain.

I love the job and the opportunities it brings. I love the boys and their rough honesty and desire to question everything. Above all, I love the opportunity to debate and discuss the Christian faith with young men who are open to truth and willing to follow it wherever it leads. The curriculum, of course, includes *Mere Christianity*, which does not immediately convince everyone; but for a good number, Lewis excites and inspires just as he did for me.

Lewis's arguments concerning miracles have come in handy in teaching philosophy as well. In fact, looking back, I find that I am only able to do this job given Lewis's help or, rather, God's grace through him to me. I know I am not the only one who has found encouragement and inspiration in his writings. I know that Lewis himself would counsel most strongly against over-reliance on one human teacher or against forgetting that the true source of all good things is God, but even given these qualifications, I can say that C. S. Lewis has been a very special instrument of grace to me.

The **Reverend Nicholas Seward** took his theological training at Durham University. As chaplain at Magdalen College School, he now has the privilege of sitting in Lewis's old pew in the college chapel, often listening to "our wonderful choir" at weekday evensong. He lives in Oxford with his wife, Hanna, and daughter, Samantha.

50

The Magic of Narnia

Mark Stibbe

One of my favorite memories from my childhood has to do with our family holidays in Scotland. Every summer we would leave the south of England and head up by car and train to the faraway reaches of the northwest isles. The little fishing village of Ullapool was our favorite holiday venue. We often stayed in a somewhat frugal little house on a high hill overlooking the expansive splendor of Loch Broom.

Those days glimmer like gold in my memory. Of course, it is always possible to indulge in idealism when remembering things past. I tend to forget the midges that feasted on our flesh every time we ventured outside, the occasional family rows over trivial issues, and the sometimes-aggravating consequences of the lack of creature comforts. But one thing I do remember fondly, and without exaggeration, is the evenings. Without television or radio, we were forced to think "outside the box," so my father came up with the idea of reading to us. And that is what he did.

Every evening my brother, sister, and I would listen to Dad reading as he moved back and forth in the rather creaky, old rocking chair. My father read us many books during those golden days. But the one that made the most lasting impact was the first he ever read to us, C. S. Lewis's *The Lion, the Witch and the Wardrobe*.

I am not entirely sure why he chose to begin our reading evenings with this particular book. We went on to The Lord of the Rings and other great works of literature. But I have a feeling that we started with Narnia because Dad had been a friend of its author. Along with several other promising Oxford undergraduates, my father had been given the privilege of meeting every week with C. S. Lewis for dinner and debate.

Whatever the reason, Dad started with *The Lion, the Witch and the Wardrobe*, and we were immediately hooked. My sister, brother, and I were held spellbound by the magic and mystery of the parallel world of Narnia. Hearing these stories stimulated many things in me personally—not the least of which was a tendency during my early years to climb into just about every wardrobe I came across. But most of all, the book triggered a yearning in my heart that I can only describe as spiritual. I wanted to be a child of destiny, like the children in the story. I wanted to be on the right side, on the side of all that is good and selfless—Aslan's side, if you will. I wanted to be a loyal servant—not easily seduced like Edmund, but totally faithful like Lucy. Deep within my heart, Lewis's classic tale gave birth to the longings that later were to result in my coming to the One whom the great Lion symbolized, Jesus Christ, and pledging the rest of my life to his service. Of all the books that I read or heard during my childhood, this one had the most influence on my life. After the Bible, it remains the book of books for me.

This account is taken from the August 2006 issue of *Christianity* magazine, a U.K. monthly publication, and is used with permission of the author.

The **Reverend Dr. Mark Stibbe** is the vicar of St. Andrews' Anglican Church, Chorleywood, and a prolific author. His books include *From Orphans to Heirs*, *Drawing Near to God*, and the best-selling *Prophetic Evangelism*. The Reverend Stibbe lives in Hertfordshire, England, with his wife, Alle, and their four children.

51

Surprised by C. S. Lewis

STEPHEN THORSON

Maleldil must be another name for Jesus Christ! Most people first read C. S. Lewis on the recommendation of a friend. I discovered Lewis while searching for science fiction in my high school library. *Out of the Silent Planet* proved to be a very different kind of science fiction. I was taken completely by surprise.

I grew up in the church and firmly believed in Jesus as the Son of God. As soon as I realized that God wanted a personal commitment, I surrendered my life to him. But the stories of the Bible didn't reach very far into my heart and imagination. Even the supernatural miracles described there seemed stale and familiar. My Christian life was sincere but intellectual, settled but devoid of real experience. I analyzed everything; my feelings were not involved.

Out of the Silent Planet marked the beginning of a great change in me. Modern literature seemed to ignore spiritual realities. Anything deeper than mundane realism was treated with skepticism or outright cynicism. But Lewis was different. Instead of showing that angels, Satan, and God were nothing but manifestations of physical matter evolving in an empty, impersonal universe, his book accepted their reality—without irony.

Immediately I asked the librarian to order the sequels. *Perelandra* was a delight! Along with travel to another planet and beautiful descriptions of an alien world, human sin was dramatized and satanic evil exposed. *That Hideous Strength* resurrected Merlin to battle a "scientific" manifestation of the devil in modern England. Both sequels wandered over the edge of science fiction into fantasy. Yet Lewis clearly believed the spiritual world to be true.

An even greater surprise was coming. In 1943 Lewis had asked readers to "await" Professor J. R. R. Tolkien's future work. I was excited to find The Lord of the Rings in our library. I discovered that Tolkien, like Lewis, dealt with deep issues—sin and death, immortality and responsibility. Both Lewis and Tolkien focused on spiritual realities without apology. Through their works I recovered a sense of wonder at creation. Even Bible stories came alive again. I experienced awe at spiritual realities, and my relationship with God became more personal and exciting. I witnessed God's healing power in myself and my family members. I learned that not only bread and wine can carry the divine to feed my soul, but trees and stones can be filled with spiritual meaning as well.

Of course, Lewis wrote more than science fiction. In *Mere Christianity* and *The Abolition of Man* he began with our universal belief in the reality of justice and beauty. Lewis brilliantly argued that denying objective standards of value only denies what makes us human. Such arguments helped form my own philosophical stance at college and in medical school. Penn State College of Medicine required classes in the humanities, and Lewis proved to be a reliable guide in courses with names such as Religion and Suffering or Philosophy of Medicine. After finishing a pediatric residency and research at the University of Virginia, I ended up with my family in Nepal, best known as the home of Mount Everest. For twenty-three years I have worked as a missionary pediatrician there, but my love for literature and theology has only increased. Lewis's arguments also helped me to earn an M.A. in theological studies in 1993, and his insights continue to help me teach theology to Nepali students part-time.

Lewis's concept of "mere Christianity"—the common ground that all Christians share with each other—has been a profound influence on my life. I thank God that he has allowed me to be part of spreading Lewis's mere Christian approach around the world. Shortly after our arrival in Nepal, church leaders encouraged a surgeon named Tom Hale to prepare a New Testament commentary, and Tom asked me to help him. Both of us worked for the United Mission to Nepal, a joint venture by mission agencies from many countries, representing the entire spectrum of theologies. Neither of us wanted to subvert the unity of the fledgling church in Nepal. My contribution was to write most of the general articles, many dealing with controversial subjects. I tried to present multiple viewpoints as fairly as possible, and I explained that differences on secondary issues should not destroy fellowship among brothers and sisters in Christ.

We discovered that this approach is rarely used. But even before our Nepali version was printed, missionaries in other countries asked to see our work. By the time an English version was published in 1996, several translations were already in progress. Now ten years later, Tom and I have just finished a companion volume on the Old Testament. Again, Lewis influenced many of my general articles for this second commentary. Discovering C. S. Lewis was a special gift. I am truly grateful for the surprise.

Stephen Thorson, M.D., works in both medicine and theology. In addition to tending sick children in Nepal and participating in medical research, he has written many articles for both the *Applied New Testament Commentary* (Kingsway U.K., Chariot Victor U.S.) and the soon-to-be-released *Applied Old Testament Commentary*. He has also authored articles on C. S. Lewis and Owen Barfield for various journals. Dr. Thorson and his wife live in Kathmandu.

52

He Turned the Intellectual Tables

Elton Trueblood

In the early days of my ministry, I believed in God and undoubtedly thought of myself as a Christian, but my theology was not evangelical. Though in my spoken ministry I often mentioned Christ, I did not emphasize his uniqueness. I spoke much of his compassion, of his emphasis upon love of the brethren, and of his faith in men, demonstrated by his recruitment of such unlikely specimens of humanity as the twelve disciples, but I tended to omit his teaching about himself and his unique relation to the Father.

Subtly and slowly the change in my message began to appear. The influences were of course numerous, but it may have been the writings of C. S. Lewis that first shocked me out of my unexamined liberalism. In reading Lewis I could not escape the conclusion that the popular view of Christ as being a teacher, and *only* a teacher, has with it a self-contradiction that cannot be resolved. I saw, in short, that conventional liberalism cannot survive rigorous and rational analysis. What Lewis and a few others made me face was the hard fact that if Christ was only a teacher, then he was a false one, since, in his teaching, he claimed to be *more*. The supposition that he taught only, or even chiefly, about loving one another is simply not true. The hard fact is that if Christ was not in a unique sense "the image of the invisible God" (Col. 1:15 KJV), as the early Christians believed, then he was certainly the arch-imposter and charlatan of history.

C. S. Lewis reached me primarily because he turned the intellectual tables. I was wholly accustomed to a world in which the sophisticates engaged in attack, while the Christians sought bravely to be on the defense, but Lewis turned this around and forced the unbeliever into a posture of defense. In *The Screwtape Letters*, Lewis, who up to that time had been an inconspicuous academician, inaugurated a new Christian strategy. I had already begun to sense that however vulnerable the Christian position may be, the position of the opposition is more vulnerable still. Once when a graduate student asked one of my professors whether the study of philosophy would help him in the support of the Christian faith, the professor replied, "No, it will not; but it will do something else of great importance—it will help you to see the weaknesses of the enemies of the faith."

The first of the weapons employed by Lewis as he began to establish a new style of dialogue was humor, a weapon then sorely needed. He had noted the striking advice of Martin Luther, "The best way to drive out the devil, if he will not yield to texts of Scripture, is to jeer and flout him, for he cannot bear scorn." In the pre-Lewis days many supposed, uncritically, that the opponents of Christianity had a monopoly upon reason, while the Christian had nothing to rely upon except faith. Lewis, to the delight of his many readers, reversed that assumption, adopting an approach reminiscent of that initiated by G. K. Chesterton. Screwtape, the archdevil, in advising his nephew about the handling of a person who is weakening in his atheism, and is even somewhat attracted to Christ, tells him, that above all, he dare not let the fellow *think*. If he thinks, says Screwtape, he will be lost to *us*.

Though Lewis helped me in many ways, he helped me most by making me face the teaching of Christ in its wholeness. If in *Screwtape* he taught me to watch for the irrationality of the opposition, it was in *Mere Christianity* that he became unanswerable. When I first read the crucial paragraph about Christ as teacher, it struck me with great force, partly because I had begun already to be skeptical about the conventional liberalism of my student days. In short, though I felt that something was wrong, it took a man of the intellectual straightforwardness of Lewis to let me see it definitely and clearly. What I saw in 1943, and have seen ever since, is that the good teacher conception is one option which Christ does not allow us to take. We can reject him; we can accept him on his terms; we cannot, with intellectual honesty, impose our own terms. The crucial paragraph is as follows:

> A man who was merely a man and said the sort of things Jesus said would not be a great moral teacher. He would either be a lunatic—on a level with the man who says he is a poached egg—or else he would be the Devil of hell. You must make your choice. Either this man was, and is, the Son of God: or else a madman or something worse. You can shut him up for a fool, you can spit at him and kill him as a demon; or you can fall at his feet and call him Lord and God. But let us not come with any patronizing nonsense about his being a great human teacher. He has not left that open to us. He did not intend to.

With that tremendous challenge to my consciousness I began to look at the Gospels in a new light. New strength came into my ministry both public and private when I saw that either I had to reject Christ and the admiring talk, or accept him on his own terms. As though illumined by a great light, I saw that he did not ask for admiration; he asked for commitment!

Taken from *While It Is Day* (Harper & Row, 1974), Elton Trueblood's autobiography; used with permission.

Educator, philosopher, theologian, and author of thirty-three books, the **Reverend Elton Trueblood** (1900–1994) was instrumental in founding the Yokefellow movement, a broadly based ecumenical "fellowship of the committed." A lifelong Quaker, Trueblood taught philosophy at Earlham College, and he reached a wider audience through his preaching and writing. He earned degrees from William Penn College, Harvard University, and Johns Hopkins University.

53

There Is So Much to Say

Michael Ward

Although I spent a large proportion of my younger years reading and rereading Lewis, and although most of my adult professional life has involved writing, tutoring, and lecturing on his works, I'm finding it difficult to complete this short article on what he has meant to me personally as a spiritual mentor.

I identify three reasons for this difficulty. The first reason is simply that there is so much to say: too much to say in a mere nine hundred words—more than can be said, really, in any number of words. My debt to Lewis is incalculable and inexpressible. There is not world enough and time to tell all I have gained from, among other things, sharing Orual's ugliness, meditating upon Agape, swimming the seas of Perelandra, mourning the loss of "H," voyaging to the Utter East, meeting the Unwelcome Fellow Traveller. No doubt, my response to every spiritual help that I have ever received from anyone is incapacitated like this. Every such help renders me eternally indebted and infinitely unable adequately to express what the help truly means. For if the help is genuinely spiritual, genuinely of the Holy Spirit, then it is a touch of God's loving hand upon my life, and its meaning can only be itself, not any summary explanation. If Lewis has helped me, which he has (a thousand times he has), it is only because the divine Helper has helped me through Lewis. Therefore I am dumbfounded. "How can I sing that Majesty which angels do admire?" as John Mason also asked in his seventeenth-century hymn.

The second reason has to do with a kind of privacy. Divine help, divine love, is not necessarily something one always wants to discuss publicly, even if one has the verbal wherewithal. If washing one's dirty linen in public is inadvisable, so too (sometimes) is displaying one's clean linen. Occasionally, the most precious and meaningful gifts we receive require no comment, no opinion; it is enough just to accept them. Jesus said, "Consider the lilies"; he didn't say, "Gild them." Is not this reticence at the heart of Lewis's classic sermon "The Weight of Glory"? When identification of the most valuable thing becomes imminent, we grow embarrassed and "betray ourselves like lovers at the mention of a name." Not everything that we prize is to be talked about.

But even where I'm not hamstrung by incapacity or privacy, I find a third difficulty in explaining what Lewis has done for me. Frankly, does it matter what Lewis *has done* for *me*? The past participle and the pronoun are danger signals. Everywhere in Lewis's works is this twofold message: God is not the God of the dead but of the living, and he is found not primarily in self-realization but self-abdication. For me, the most fatal word in the spiritual life is *encore*— the desire to live in the past—and the most blessed thing in the spiritual life is self-defeat—our pilgrimage through the green valley of humiliation. What have Lewis's works *done* for *me*? They've revealed that present *doing* is more important than cut-and-dried *done*, and that *God* loving me is more important than *me* loving him.

However, the nature of this book requires a degree of autobiography from its contributors, and so I should perhaps point out that I have learned one peculiarly personal thing from Lewis as a result of the fact that the path of my own life has, in certain ways, led me to tread in a number of his footsteps. Like Lewis, I read English at Oxford. Like him, I lived at The Kilns (for three years, between 1996 and 1999). Like him, I then transferred to Cambridge (where I worked as Chaplain of Peterhouse, 2004–2007). It so fell out, by a strange concatenation of circumstances, that I even ended up sitting for my Ph.D. dissertation defense in Lewis's old rooms at Magdalene College, his framed picture looking down at me as I defended my thesis. I mention these things not in the slightest bit because I view myself as Elisha to his Elijah, but because these vestiges of his experience have revealed to me from the inside some of the trials and constraints that his life's course brought him.

Like Lewis, I know firsthand the temptations to vanity and pretense that accompany an Oxbridge education. I know firsthand how freezing cold and miserably damp his bedroom can be in mid-December! I know firsthand the pressure of living in an Oxbridge college as a senior member and of having to face the Fellowship day in and day out, a few of whose members would contentedly see one fall, and how such pressure can incline one to compromise one's Christian witness. From these vantage points, I can observe how remarkably well Lewis lived his life; he did not allow his academic distinction to make him proud or highfalutin; he did not let domestic difficulties of various kinds—not just freezing temperatures, but also some very testing relationships—turn him into an ingrate; he did not trim his faith to suit his own comfort. Not that he himself was especially strong or heroic or virtuous by his own nature, but he rested in Christ. And that example is encouraging. I take heart from what Lewis shows to be possible.

Michael Ward lectures widely on Lewis at universities and events both in the U.K. and abroad. He worked as research assistant to Walter Hooper on *C. S. Lewis: A Companion and Guide* and has published numerous articles and reviews. His most recent book, *Planet Narnia: The Seven Heavens in the Imagination of C. S. Lewis* (Oxford University Press), demonstrates how Lewis's knowledge of medieval cosmology provides the subtle key to the seven novels.

54

Lewis Was the Joshua Flattening the Walls of My Disbelief

John C. Wright

When I meet Clive Staples Lewis in heaven, I shall certainly shake his hand, for he saved my soul. Oh, I suppose that statement is not quite right. Divine grace—nothing else—saves souls, but the door is not open to the person who does not knock, and nothing will answer before a person asks. In my case it was Jack Lewis, among others, who talked me into knocking and asking.

My atheism was lifelong, deep-rooted, and implacably hostile. It was Lewis who convinced me that there was a sufficient intellectual basis for Christianity for it to be taken seriously.

I was an apologist for atheism as Lewis was an apologist for faith. At my command were reason and wit, solid syllogism and airily clever turns of phrase. I was as perfect and well-defended a fortress of the intellect as the natural reason of a human being could erect. Strange as it sounds, it was this very strength, this intellectual integrity, which made me an atheist. My sense of honesty would not allow me to believe childish fairy tales—which I thought Christianity to be.

Ironically, what C. S. Lewis did was to use a children's fairy tale to show me that Christianity was not a fairy tale at all, and his powers of reason showed me the common sense of it, the logic of faith. I cannot emphasize how important this is. An atheist is never convinced of the truth of our faith all at one blow. Even the walls of Jericho, flattened by a miracle, did not fall down until the Israelites had patiently circled it for seven days, blowing the horns and proclaiming. My life was just such a wall; Jack Lewis was the Joshua blowing.

How did Lewis go about this? First and foremost, he did this by living the Christian life. Christianity informed Lewis's books, even his children's books and science fiction, in a way that was natural. Because he honestly believed, his honesty came across even when he was not trying to make a point about his belief. I read his Narnia books at a time when there were very few other fantasy books written, and there is many a small boy with a profound thirst for the fantastic. The simple heroisms, the beloved beauty of those books, planted the love of tales in my heart. And no one who loves a good tale can reject the Greatest Story Ever Told forever.

Second, he did this by being a Christian man of letters—learned, patient, and above all, logical. I read with great interest—as an enemy would scan intercepted battle plans—the arguments of Lewis's apologetics. Being an intellectual, I had a greater interest in these than in his tales. Surprisingly, I found myself an ally in his *The Abolition of Man*, for I had been convinced for many years of the philosophical position of the objectivity of morals. No truly moral person can regard morality as relative. So another section of my wall was undermined, for I found my hated enemies, the Christians, talking plain common sense while my alleged allies in the secular realm were talking errant nonsense.

Third, he did this by displaying, in all modesty, the wisdom of a Christian sage. After reading Lewis's purely apologetic works like "God in the Dock," I had developed a taste for Lewis. To indulge this taste, I read his more purely academic works: *A Preface to "Paradise Lost"* and *The Discarded Image*. There was something in his approach, his humility, and his charity that I liked. What also impressed me was not merely the humility but also the reasonableness of his writings. It was not until my logical objections to the mysteries of faith were quieted that the Voice from beyond the edge of the world could speak to me.

Beauty also was one of the divine weapons that God used to surprise and pierce my unbelieving heart. The scene in *The Silver Chair* where Puddleglum, the Marsh-wiggle, his memory fogged by the enchantments of a witch, announces that he is ready to live and die as a Narnian would even if there is no Narnia, is not merely a profound statement of the role of Christian faith during moments of doubt; it is also a stirring moment of heroism. There is something becoming and satisfying in heroism, particularly coming from such an ungainly character as the gloomy Puddleglum, something infinitely right and proper. When we see it, our hearts know its rightness.

There is a similar scene in *That Hideous Strength*, when Mark Studdock, a young intellectual of the shallow, agnostic bent, is brought by the servants of an inhuman scientific tyranny into the "Objectification Room," where he is confronted by distorted images, nothing at right angles, an environment where nothing is proper. He is asked, upon pain of death, to trample a cross, a symbol that should mean nothing to him, but his human sympathy for the image of the innocent man who died on that cross steels his will. He does not yet know God, not in this scene, but he has a sense of rightness, a sense of proportion, which is implanted in all human hearts. That sense of proportion is another divine weapon.

These and other weapons C. S. Lewis handled like a man inspired. After my conversion, the apologetic arguments of Puddleglum or Mark Studdock, the heroism of Christianity, its fitness in proportion, were already in my spiritual arsenal, placed there by C. S. Lewis.

The most comforting thought of all for me, which I had experienced in the highest peak of my religious ecstasy, was the thought uttered by Uncle Screwtape in Lewis's *The Screwtape Letters*. The superior tempter mentions that recent converts are susceptible to think, like newlywed bridegrooms, that the infatuation of new love is the steady state of true love. I was on my guard against this, and my faith did not falter even when my emotions changed; it had already been put on a footing more rational, less personal, less to do with me and my feelings, and all to do with God and my service toward him.

Uncle Screwtape also warned me not to look askance at the off-key hymnist in the squeaky boots one pew over. I am sure we all sound equally out of harmony to heaven, but equally cute, and we all sound equally hideous to hell when we sing our thanksgivings.

I give thanks for Jack Lewis.

An acclaimed author of science fiction and fantasy novels, **John C. Wright** converted from atheism to Christianity at age forty-two. A retired attorney, Wright lives with his wife and three children in Virginia, where he also works as a technical writer.

55

Shadow Mentor

Philip Yancey

I first encountered C. S. Lewis while attending a Bible college in the South at a time when neither the college nor I was in very healthy shape. Drifting along between presidents, the school had filled faculty rosters with furloughing missionaries and other temporary professors, who were treading in waters all too deep. And I, in recovery from a fundamentalist church upbringing and with the arrogance of immaturity, looked on the school with disdain. I took a devilish delight in pricking holes in the faith of my classmates and stumping professors with questions they could not answer.

As I recall, I read Lewis's Space Trilogy first. Though perhaps not his best work, it had an undermining effect on me. He made the supernatural so believable that I could not help wondering, *What if it's really true? What if there is a God and an afterlife, and what if supernatural forces really are operating behind the scenes on this planet and in my life?* The tremors strengthened into an earthquake as I went on to read *Mere Christianity* and *The Problem of Pain*, which dismantled my defenses and convicted me of the sin of pride.

I was attending college in the late 1960s, just a few years after Lewis's death in 1963. I ordered more of his books from secondhand bookshops in England because many had not yet made it across the Atlantic. I wrestled with them as with a debate opponent and reluctantly felt myself drawn, as Lewis himself had, kicking and screaming all the way into the kingdom of God. Since then he has been a constant companion, a kind of shadow mentor who sits beside me urging me to improve my writing style, my thinking, my vision.

Ultimately I became a full-time writer and have written some twenty books. Before writing any book, first I laboriously go through all of Lewis's to see what he said about the topic. For instance, my latest book examines the topic of prayer. I found, not to my surprise, that virtually every question I have about prayer, Lewis anticipated and commented on. In personal letters, in essays, in stray paragraphs, and in an entire book (*Letters to Malcolm: Chiefly on Prayer*) he grappled with the fundamental issues of why God would value that singular activity and what difference it makes to an omniscient being.

As my shadow mentor, Lewis has taught me a style of approach that I try to follow in all my writings. To quote William James, "In the metaphysical and religious sphere, articulate reasons are cogent for us only when our inarticulate feelings of reality have already been impressed in favor of the same conclusion." In other words, we rarely accept a logical argument unless it fits an intuitive sense of reality. The writer's challenge is to nurture that intuitive sense—as Lewis had done for me with his Space Trilogy before I encountered his apologetics. Lewis himself converted to Christianity only after sensing that it corresponded to his deepest longings, his *Sehnsucht*. Though a powerful apologist who could be fearsome in personal debate, in his writings Lewis romanced rather than browbeat readers toward the faith. He honored the written word for its freedom-respecting quality. In so doing he reflected God's own style of revelation, not through overpowering images but through the Word, that most risky and rejectable form of communication.

Yet Lewis's background of atheism and doubt gave him a lifelong understanding of and compassion for readers who would not accept his words. He had engaged in a gallant tug-of-war with God, only to find that the God on the other end of the rope was entirely different from what he had imagined. Likewise, I had to overcome an image of God badly marred by an angry and legalistic church. I fought hard against a cosmic bully only to discover a God of grace and mercy.

The love that becomes a god may also become a demon, wrote Lewis in *The Four Loves*. For example, a mother may suffocate her child with love; out of love for country a patriot may commit war crimes. And the church, called to dispense the highest form of love, stands in constant danger of corrupting *agape* into its opposite. The keys of the kingdom become tools of power (think Crusades and Inquisition) rather than invitation. Lewis affirmed the writer's obligation to expose such a danger. Humility and honesty are our only sure defenses.

He wrote in *A Grief Observed*, "My idea of God is not a divine idea. It has to be shattered time after time. He shatters it Himself. He is the great iconoclast. Could we not almost say that this shattering is one of the marks of His presence? The Incarnation is the supreme example; it leaves all previous ideas of the Messiah in ruins." That book, conceived after his wife died a most cruel death from bone cancer, unsettles some readers. Lewis had dealt with theodicy philosophically in *The Problem of Pain*, but tidy arguments melted away as he watched the process of bodily devastation in the woman he loved. I believe the two books should be read together, for the combination of ultimate answers and existential agony reflects the biblical pattern. The cross saved the world, but, oh, at what cost!

In contrast to some Christians, Lewis saw the world as a place worth saving. Unlike the monastics of the Middle Ages and the legalists of modern times, he saw no need to withdraw and deny all pleasures. He loved a stiff drink, a puff on the pipe, a gathering of friends, a Wagnerian opera, a walk in the fields of Oxford. The pleasures in life are indeed good, just not good enough; in *The Weight of Glory* he says that they are "only the scent of a flower we have not found, the echo of a tune we have not heard, news from a country we have never yet visited." Our desires are too small, our vision too limited.

I found in Lewis that rare and precarious balance of embracing the world while not idolizing it. For all its defects, this planet bears marks of the original design, traces of Beauty and Joy that both recall and anticipate the Creator's intent. Alone of modern authors, Lewis taught me to anticipate heaven: "We are half-hearted creatures, fooling about with drink and sex and ambition when infinite joy is offered us, like an ignorant child who wants to go on making mud pies in a slum because he cannot imagine what is meant by the offer of a holiday at the sea" ("The Weight of Glory"). We need not deny the world to attain heaven, yet we dare not love the world so much that we miss its consummation.

Finally, Lewis affirmed my calling as a writer. We live lonely lives, those of us who make a living by playing with words. I find it hard to write if someone shares the same room with me. More, any impact I have on others will be vicarious. When I write, I am not actively caring for the poor, ministering to AIDS victims, feeding the hungry, or even conversing about spiritual matters. "We read to know that we are not alone," said one of Lewis's students in the movie *Shadowlands*. Yes, and we write in desperate hope that we are not alone. Lewis proved to me that this most lonely act can make a difference. As one who was changed—literally, dramatically, permanently—by an Oxford don who spent most of his life as a bachelor, rarely traveled, and felt more at home with books than people, I have learned to trust that God can use my own feeble efforts to connect with readers out there somewhere, most of whom I will never meet.

I doubt C. S. Lewis ever anticipated that almost half a century after his death several million people each year would buy one of his dozens of books still in print or that Disney Studios would release movies based on Narnia with spin-off products available in every shopping mall. If informed of that fact during his life, he would likely have shrunk back in alarm. We writers are not Nouns, he used to say. We are mere adjectives, pointing to the great Noun of truth. Lewis did that, faithfully and masterfully, and because he did so, many thousands have come to know and love that Noun. Including me.

Philip Yancey writes on spiritual themes. Many of his twenty books have won awards: *The Jesus I Never Knew*, *What's So Amazing About Grace?*, *Where Is God When It Hurts?*, *Church: Why Bother?*, *Disappointment with God*, *Soul Survivor: How My Faith Survived the Church*, *Rumors of Another World*, and *Prayer: Does It Make a Difference?* are just a few. He has also written, with Dr. Paul Brand: *Fearfully and Wonderfully Made*, *In His Image*, and *The Gift of Pain*. He and his wife, Janet, live in Colorado, where he has climbed all fifty-four of the 14,000-foot peaks in the state. Janet has accompanied him on most of these climbs.

Books by C. S. Lewis

Letters, Diaries, Autobiographical Books

All My Road before Me: The Diary of C. S. Lewis, 1922–1927
Surprised by Joy: The Shape of My Early Life
A Grief Observed
Letters of C. S. Lewis
Letters to an American Lady
They Stand Together: The Letters of C. S. Lewis to Arthur Greeves
Letters to Children
The Latin Letters of C. S. Lewis: C. S. Lewis and Don Giovanni Calabria
The Collected Letters of C. S. Lewis, Volumes I, II, III[1]
Yours, Jack: Spiritual Direction from C. S. Lewis[2]

Fiction and Poetry

Novels and Stories

Boxen: The Imaginative World of the Young C. S. Lewis

1. In the three volumes of the *Collected Letters*, Walter Hooper has exhaustively gathered every letter available at the time of publication, including those contained in the five books of letters listed above them.

2. In this one volume, Paul F. Ford has culled and thematically arranged selections from the *Collected Letters*.

The "Ransom" (or "Cosmic" or "Space") Trilogy

Out of the Silent Planet

Perelandra

That Hideous Strength: A Modern Fairy-tale for Grown-ups

Till We Have Faces: A Myth Retold

The Dark Tower: And Other Stories

Fairy Tales (The Chronicles of Narnia)

The Lion, the Witch and the Wardrobe

Prince Caspian

The Voyage of the "Dawn Treader"

The Silver Chair

The Horse and His Boy

The Magician's Nephew

The Last Battle

Speculative/Theological Fiction

The Pilgrim's Regress

The Screwtape Letters

The Great Divorce: A Dream

Poetry

Spirits in Bondage

Dymer

Poems

The Collected Poems of C. S. Lewis[3]

Narrative Poems

3. Though not commercially available in the U.S., *Collected Poems* gathers the contents of *Poems* and *Spirits in Bondage*, along with a previously unavailable "Miscellany" of seventeen poems.

Popular Theology

The Problem of Pain
The Abolition of Man
George MacDonald: An Anthology
Miracles: A Preliminary Study
Mere Christianity
Reflections on the Psalms
The Four Loves
Letters to Malcolm: Chiefly on Prayer

Essays, Addresses

The Weight of Glory and Other Addresses
The World's Last Night: And Other Essays
They Asked for a Paper: Papers and Addresses
Screwtape Proposes a Toast: And Other Pieces
Christian Reflections
God in the Dock: Essays on Theology and Ethics
On Stories: And Other Essays on Literature
Present Concerns
Essay Collection: Faith, Christianity and the Church
Essay Collection: Literature, Philosophy and Short Stories[4]

Scholarly Works

The Allegory of Love: A Study in Medieval Tradition
The Personal Heresy: A Controversy
A Preface to "Paradise Lost"
English Literature in the Sixteenth Century Excluding Drama
Studies in Words

4. Though not commercially available in the United States, the two volumes of *Essay Collections* represent the most complete and convenient gathering of Lewis's essays and include nearly all essays in the eight books listed above them.

An Experiment in Criticism
The Discarded Image: An Introduction to Medieval and Renaissance Literature
Studies in Medieval and Renaissance Literature
Spenser's Images of Life
Selected Literary Essays
On Stories and Other Essays on Literature
Studies in Words

Quotations, Selections of Readings

A Mind Awake: An Anthology of C. S. Lewis
The Joyful Christian: 127 Readings from C. S. Lewis
The Business of Heaven: Daily Readings from C. S. Lewis
Visionary Christian: 131 Readings from C. S. Lewis
The Essential C. S. Lewis
The Quotable Lewis
Readings for Meditation and Reflection
A Year with C. S. Lewis
Words to Live By: A Guide for the Merely Christian

Books about C. S. Lewis

While nearly impossible to keep up with the variety and number of books about C. S. Lewis, the works on the following list provide the most frequent, consistent, and thorough help.

C. S. Lewis: A Companion and Guide by Walter Hooper. The single most important work on C. S. Lewis to date.

The C. S. Lewis Reader's Encyclopedia edited by Jeffrey D. Schultz and John G. West Jr. A useful guide covering all of Lewis's published writing by current scholars.

The C. S. Lewis Index by Janine Goffar. An incredibly helpful concordance of ideas and quotes and their sources.

The Quotable Lewis edited by Wayne Martindale and Jerry Root. The best single-volume gathering of quotes, alphabetically arranged.

Companion to Narnia by Paul F. Ford. A masterful and encyclopedic guide not only to every important figure and event in Narnia, but also to key concepts to Lewis's imaginative thought.

Jack: A Life of C. S. Lewis by George Sayer. Written by a former student, this remains perhaps the best biography to date.

The Company They Keep: C. S. Lewis and J. R. R. Tolkien as Writers in Community by Diana Pavlac Glyer. A comprehensive, meticulously researched, and eminently readable look at Lewis and Tolkien's writing group the Inklings.

Brothers and Friends: An Intimate Portrait of C. S. Lewis by Warren H. Lewis. Warnie's diary contains a number of unique insights into life with Lewis.

Remembering C. S. Lewis edited by James Como. Reminiscences from a number of Lewis's key friends and colleagues. Also contains Walter Hooper's 100+ page definitive "Bibliography of the Writings of C. S. Lewis."

C. S. Lewis: Images of His World by Douglas R. Gilbert and Clyde S. Kilby. Photos and text from Lewis's whole life, including glimpses of his childhood, Oxford, Cambridge, his walking tours, and several of his friends.

Questions for Discussion and Reflection

1. Randy Alcorn says (on p. 41), "Aslan unlocked the mystery of the 'fear of God,' which had been hard for me to harmonize with the love of God." What do you think C. S. Lewis meant when he says through Mr. Beaver to Lucy in *The Lion, the Witch and the Wardrobe*, "He is not safe, but he is good"? How does that help our understanding of God?

2. Mary DeKonty Applegate recounts that a remark from her brother that he was praying for the "sweet spirit of Christ" (p. 44) jump-started her spiritual journey. Who or what influenced your spiritual growth? What were major difficulties for you?

3. David Downing writes, "Lewis intended for his fiction to re-energize his readers' spiritual imaginations" (p. 100). Do you find Lewis's Space Trilogy helpful in unfettering *your* ideas of heaven, hell, angels, or God? Have you encountered any "eldils" recently? What ways has Lewis's writing inspired your creativity?

4. Martha Atkins Emmert reflects what many followers of Christ experience—"floundering in my own sea of need" (p. 109). What faith-building truths have you found from C. S. Lewis or other writers that have aided your pilgrimage? How has Lewis

pointed you toward your own need of God or shown you how God fills those needs?

5. Janine Goffar was raised in a Christian home but had a "borrowed religion" until C. S. Lewis helped her make it her own (p. 118). Can you relate experiences in your life when a "borrowed religion" transformed into real Joy?

6. A fellow student challenged John C. Lennox that his faith in God was "purely culturally dependent" (p. 162), that he was simply a product of his Irish heritage. How did C. S. Lewis help him see that the Christian worldview was not an "irrational leap in the dark"? And how does Lewis help you make sense of faith?

7. Lawrence Macala says that as a convinced atheist "science had become my god" (p. 166). He hoped science would lead him to truth. Francis S. Collins tells a similar story (pp. 79–80). What brought him to doubt his atheism and to become "re-enchanted by the Truth" with a capital "T"? What resources does Lewis offer us to hold a rational faith in a scientific and often unbelieving world?

8. Both Pierce Pettis and Anne Rice admire C. S. Lewis's intellectual honesty and being "profound in such simple, concise language" (p. 182). What examples or metaphors in Lewis's work help you embrace the faith or explain it more clearly to others?

9. Thousands have been drawn to Christ or returned to faith through Lewis's popular fairy tales. Stephen Savage, Nicholas Seward, Mark Stibbe and others relate how they were charmed by the supernatural in the Chronicles of Narnia. Which of the seven Narnia tales "hooked" you, and why?

10. Elton Trueblood applauds C. S. Lewis's "intellectual straightforwardness" (p. 203). Jesus was who he said he was; one must accept him on his terms or reject him. One must choose. One can't dismiss him as simply a great teacher. Where are you on the spiritual path? What are we to make of Jesus Christ, and, more to the point (as Lewis said), what is he to make of us?

Mary Anne Phemister is a docent at the Marion E. Wade Center, the world's foremost archive and repository of material relating to C. S. Lewis and other like-minded authors including G. K. Chesterton, J. R. R. Tolkien, Dorothy L. Sayers, and George MacDonald. She and her pianist husband, Bill, live in Wheaton, Illinois.

Andrew Lazo holds an M.A. in literature from Rice University, where he was Jacob K. Javits Fellow in the Humanities. He teaches literature at the University of Houston and is an independent speaker and scholar on the life and works of C. S. Lewis. A frequent presenter for the C. S. Lewis Foundation, Andrew gives seminars, lectures, and retreats on Lewis for people of all ages around the United States and in the United Kingdom.